A Guide to
Observation and Participation

In the Classroom

A Guide to
Observation and Participation
In the Classroom

Arthea J. S. Reed
Verna E. Bergemann

University of North Carolina at Asheville

DPG

The Dushkin Publishing Group, Inc.

Printed in the United States of America

International Standard Book Number (ISBN) 0-87967-065-0

First Printing

The Dushkin Publishing Group, Inc., Sluice Dock, Guilford, Connecticut 06437

INTRODUCTION

A Guide to Observation and Participation In the Classroom is written for you, the student. It is designed to help you not only bridge the gap between the world of the student and the world of the teacher, but also to help you connect the world of theory to the world of practice. You will learn to view students, schools, and teachers as a teacher would and you must develop and practice the skills and techniques of effective teaching in order to perfect them. This *Guide to Observation and Participation In the Classroom* will facilitate these tasks.

Because observing teachers and students and classroom situations to gain knowledge and understanding of the teaching profession comes first, the first three chapters of this book deal with observation. Throughout each of these chapters you will find numerous forms for recording observations that have been completed by student observers in the field. These should give you an example of how to use the forms which appear at the end of this book, numbered to coincide with the forms in the chapter.

Once you have had the opportunity to reflect on your observations, the second section of this guide provides you with many of the tools that will help organize the classroom and suggests techniques used by effective teachers. Chapter four explains the importance of classroom participation during teacher training. In subsequent chapters we discuss preteaching, planning, tutoring, teaching small groups, and teaching large groups.

Finally, following the chapters you will find copies of all of the observation and participation forms and instruments that have been used in the book. These can be removed and duplicated for your use. Each of these has been extensively field-tested by college and university students over a period of seven years.

The authors of this *Guide to Observation and Participation In the Classroom* hope that as you complete and reflect on each of these activities, you will strengthen your resolve to teach and deepen your understanding, knowledge, and skills of effective teaching.

Arthea J. S. Reed
Verna E. Bergemann
Asheville, NC

CONTENTS

III FORMS 97

PART I

Observing In the Schools

1

OBSERVING TEACHERS

Observation is one effective means of learning how certain teaching methods are employed in the schools, how classrooms are organized, and how students respond to the classroom environment. This guide will provide the future teacher with information on the processes of observation and participation in general and with specific forms that can be used in specific classroom situations.

ANECDOTAL OBSERVATION

Anecdotal observations focus on exactly what occurs in a classroom or on what a child does or says in a specific situation over a limited period of time. Anecdotal observations are informally recorded in narrative in an observer's observation log. As much as possible, they are an exact description of a classroom event or incident. Anecdotal observations are simple to do. Observers need no training, but must follow the rules of all good observation: (1) the observer must observe the entire sequence or event, (2) goals, limits, or guidelines must be set, (3) the observation should be recorded completely and carefully, and (4) observation must be as objective as possible.

Observing the Entire Event or Sequence

Typically, anecdotal observations deal with what might be called minimal situations. The observer watches one child or one teaching or management technique for a specified period of time over several observations. This allows the observer to make dated notes while focusing attention on a single element or individual in the classroom or school. The minimal situation technique narrows the observer's focus to one event. Trying to follow too many elements of the classroom at one time usually leads to incomplete observation of all of them. Focusing on too much caused Sarah and Steve (see chapter 2 of the text *In the Classroom: An Introduction to Education,* pp. 50–53) to make inaccurate judgments.

SAMPLE FORM 1

ANECDOTAL RECORD FORM FOR
OBSERVING TEACHERS OR INSTRUCTIONAL EVENTS—1

Name of Observer: <u>Karen Susan Richie</u>

Date and Time of Observation: <u>December 2, 19— 10:30 a.m.</u>

Length of Observation: <u>Approximately 35 minutes</u>

Person and/or Event Observed: <u>Mrs. Menotti teaching a reading lesson</u>

Grade Level and/or Subject: <u>Second grade, reading</u>

Objective of Observation: <u>To determine how Mrs. Menotti works with individuals</u> <u>within the reading group</u>

Instructions to the Observer: As completely and accurately as possible, describe the person or the event. If appropriate, include direct quotes and descriptions of the location or individual. Try to avoid making judgments.

Mrs. Menotti called the red group, the Space Invaders, to the reading corner at the right rear of the classroom. "Be sure to bring your free reading books with you, Space Invaders," said Mrs. M.

I move over to the reading corner so I can better observe the group. The reading corner is next to the window and the students' chairs are arranged in a circle. Mrs. M's chair is a large, wooden slat rocking chair next to the bookcase. Her chair is in the circle of chairs.

The students get their books from their desks. Joey says, "Mrs. M., I finished my book and I need to see if I can find it in the library." "Is it in the classroom library, Joey?" Mrs. M. asks. "Yes." "O.K., you can look for it Joey. Just don't disturb the rest of us while you're looking."

Once all the students (except Joey) are seated in the circle, Mrs. M. takes out her own book. She says to Joey, "Have you found it?" "Not yet," Joey replies. "Well, join us while I read and you can go back to the library and look afterward."

Mrs. M. asks Melody if she can remember what happened last in the story. (I can't see the title of the book Mrs. M. is reading from. I must remember to ask her later.) Melody begins to tell the story. Melody talks so quietly that it is difficult to hear her. Mrs. M. asks the other students some questions. "Sandy, can you remember what happened to the rabbit when the boy got sick?" "They took him from the nursery," Sandy says. "They were afraid the rabbit was comintated [sic]," says Maggie. "Do you mean 'contaminated'?" asks Mrs. M. Maggie looks at her hands. "Yes," says Maggie very quietly. "Very good, Maggie. That's right," says Mrs. M. Maggie looks up and smiles. "Why do you think they were afraid the rabbit might be contaminated, Sean?" Sean replies, "Well, he was stuffed and the boy is real sick, so the rabbit might have germs." "Very good, Sean," says Mrs. M.

She begins to read. All the students are listening. After each page she shows the children the illustration on the page. She reads one page and turns to the next and Sean says, "Hey, Mrs. M., you forgot to show us the picture." "There isn't one on that page, Sean."

She reads for about ten minutes and asks, "Do you like the story, Abbie?" Abbie nods her head. "Why do you like it?" she asks. "I like the boy and I want him to get well and get his rabbit back. It's sad," says Abbie. "Do you like sad stories, Mark?" "Yes, sometimes," says Mark. "Is the story you've been reading sad?" "No," Mark says. "Would you tell us about your book, Mark, please?" Mark does. It's the story of a space trip to Mars taken by a little boy. Melody says, "Did he really take that trip, Mark? I think it was all a dream." "No," says Mark, "It was real." "How do you know, Mark?" asks Sean. Mark says back very loudly, "Because the book doesn't say it's a dream." "Yeah," says Melody, "but in the beginning of the book he's in bed, and in the end he's back in his bed." Mark is quiet. Mrs. M. smiles, "When you read a story you can decide for yourself what it means. If Melody thinks it was a dream, that's O.K., even if Mark doesn't think it's a dream. Why don't you read it, Melody, and see if you still think it's a dream." Melody does not answer. Mrs. M. turns to Joey and says, "Joey, do you want to get your book so that you can tell us about it after Abbie tells us about hers?" [Karen's observation continues until the reading group is over.]

Setting Goals, Limits, or Guidelines

As with all observation, the observer must know the objective of the observation. What is it the observer hopes to see in the classroom or school? The observer may simply want to explore how the teacher communicates with individual students, as Karen observed in the sample anecdotal record form for observing teachers. Another way to do this is to keep a simple anecdotal record of student-teacher communication. The observer writes down as accurately as possible all the communication that occurs between the teacher and one student during a specified period of time. Since one important element of an effective school is good communication, examining how the teacher communicates with individual students can reveal a great deal about whether or not the classroom is effective. Of course, several observations of this student and other students would be required before a judgment could be made.

SAMPLE FORM 2

ANECDOTAL TEACHER-STUDENT
INTERACTION FORM

Name of Observer: Karen Susan Richie

Date and Time of Observation: December 2, 19— 10:30 a.m.

Length of Observation: Approximately 35 minutes

Name of Teacher: Mrs. Menotti

Name of Student: Joey

Grade Level and/or Subject: Second grade

Objective of Observation: How does Mrs. Menotti interact with an individual student?

Instructions to the Observer: As completely and accurately as possible, describe the interactions between the teacher and one selected student. Include direct quotes and descriptions of the teacher and the student, including facial expressions, gestures, and voice quality. However, be careful to avoid making judgments.

Time	Teacher	Student
10:36	*Mrs. Menotti*	*Joey* "Mrs. M., I finished my book and I need to see if I can find it in the library." Joey calls out very loudly across the room to Mrs. M.
	Mrs. M. smiles at Joey and makes a "sh" sign. She looks him directly in the eye, "Is it in the classroom library, Joey?"	
		"Yes." Joey answers much more quietly and smiles back at Mrs. M.
	"O.K., you can look for it, Joey. Just don't disturb the rest of us while you're looking."	
		Joey moves quietly to the classroom library behind Mrs. M's rocking chair and begins to search.

Perhaps the observer might want to examine another element of an effective school, rewarding student achievement. The observer might use the anecdotal recording technique to determine how the teacher and the school reward the students for academic achievement. To do this, the observer simply examines the classroom and the school building for signs that student achievement has been rewarded, and lists these in the observational log.

SAMPLE FORM 3

ANECDOTAL RECORD FORM FOR OBSERVING TEACHERS OR INSTRUCTIONAL EVENTS—2

Name of Observer: James McClure

Date and Time of Observation: January 6, 19— 9:35 a.m.

Length of Observation: 30 minutes

Person and/or Event Observed: Mr. Martine's classroom

Grade Level and/or Subject: Eighth grade, Lang. Arts and Social Studies

Objective of Observation: To determine how school/classroom environment promotes student achievement

Instructions to the Observer: As completely and accurately as possible, describe the person or the event. If appropriate, include direct quotes and descriptions of the location or the individual. Try to avoid making judgments.

1. student work displayed on bulletin boards in hallways, 2. students who won speech contest mentioned over intercom during morning announcements, 3. teacher mentions a student who won a Boy Scout honor, 4. classroom bulletin board displays students' writing from last week, 5. students are working on putting together a desktop computer publication of their writing, 6. books children have written and illustrated are on check-out shelf at the rear of the room, 7. student art work related to social studies unit is displayed on the wall above the windows.

Recording Completely and Carefully

Anecdotal records require the careful recording of events over a specified period of time. It might be useful for the observer to do two or more recordings, since it is impossible to write down everything that occurs in just one observation. For example, in observing one child, he might record her activities every five minutes for an hour. Later he might record her activities every five minutes for another hour. It is important for the observer to write down exactly what the child is doing, avoiding any judgments of her behavior.

A schedule is also important if the goal of the observer is to examine classroom organization. For example, if an observer is watching grouping techniques in a classroom, she might record the formal and informal grouping patterns every 30 minutes.

An anecdotal observation like this reveals an interesting grouping pattern in Mr. Hanks's classroom that observation of everything in the classroom might not.

SAMPLE FORM 4

ANECDOTAL RECORD FORM
FOR GROUPING PATTERNS

Name of Observer: Sylvia Rodriguez

Date and Time of Observation: October 29, 19— 8:45 a.m.

Length of Observation: All day

Person and/or Event Observed: Mr. Hanks

Grade Level and/or Subject: Fifth grade

Objective of Observation: To examine grouping patterns

Instructions to the Observer: As completely and accurately as possible, describe the patterns. If appropriate, include direct quotes and descriptions of locations or individuals. Try to avoid making judgments.

8:45 - reading groups meet with teacher; all of the children in each group read in turn from the same-level basal reader; three different level readers are used by the five groups; the teacher reinforces skills by calling the children's attention to words on a flip chart.

9:15 - math groups in which all the children are working on different kinds of math problems; two groups are doing long division, another multiplication, another fractions (population of the math groups differs from population of the reading groups—i.e., Sarah Jane is in the fraction math group, but was reading from the lowest level reader).

9:45 - children continue in math groups; three larger groups have divided into pairs; the pairs are helping each other complete the homework assignments listed for each group on the chalkboard; Mr. Hanks has spent all his time working with the multiplication group, the only group not now working in pairs, except for a few minutes to answer the questions of the other groups.

10:15 - recess—children form their own groups; a group of 10 boys is playing soccer, a group of 7 girls is skipping rope, two girls are reading, a group of 4 boys is playing chase, two girls are walking, one girl is sitting with Mr. Hanks.

10:45 - social studies groups—students are investigating different aspects of the community; the children seem to know their assignments; each student has a folder which was picked up at the front of the room when Mr. Hanks announced it was time for social studies; the students go to the supply cabinet or the bookshelves when they need materials; they go up to Mr. Hanks's desk with questions (Mr. Hanks does not work with these groups, but observes their activities from his desk).

11:45 - lunch (did not observe).

12:00 - all students participate in a class meeting with Mr. Hanks about the Halloween party (the class president presides over this large group); students sit in a large circle; they raise their hands when they want to make a point; Mr. Hanks records each point made on a flip chart; he only speaks to redirect the discussion to other students.

12:30 - students line up by row, as called by Mr. Hanks, to go to music; one row of mostly boys is not allowed to leave until they have quieted down; they do not have their materials put away and are busy talking; it takes about 3 minutes for them to get organized and quiet; then Mr. Hanks lets them leave.

2:15 - small groups participating in a variety of classroom management chores (i.e., one group is picking up papers and cleaning desks, tables, and floor; another group is rearranging the chairs and adjusting the blinds; a third group is putting papers in students' folders; a fourth group is collecting books and placing them on the bookshelves).

STRUCTURED OBSERVATIONS

Structured observations follow a specific format. As in anecdotal observations, one should follow the rules of good observation. Unlike anecdotal observations, structured observations are formal and require that specific information be recorded. Structured observations include: rank ordering, coding, checklists, interviews (discussed in this chapter), profiles, and sociograms (discussed in chapter three).

Rank Ordering

One easy, nonjudgmental way to examine what has been observed in the classroom is to organize the observations in order of frequency. Many things can be rank ordered. For example, it is possible to rank order the following techniques employed by the teacher: instructional techniques (lecturing, discussion, small group work, individual work, etc.), grouping patterns, management approaches, methods of discipline, types of questions, and types of assignments. If Karen, in the sample anecdotal record form for observing teachers or instructional events, had been observing grouping patterns in Mrs. Menotti's classroom over the period of a week, she could have rank ordered the grouping patterns by frequency of occurrence. To do this, of course, she would first have to know what types of groups she had seen.

SAMPLE FORM 5

OBSERVATION FORM FOR RANK ORDERING

Name of Observer: Karen Susan Richie

Date and Time of Observation: Week of November 4, 19—

Length of Observation: One week

Techniques or Types Observed: Mrs. Menotti - Grouping Patterns

Grade Level and/or Subject: Second grade

Objective of Observation: To examine grouping patterns

Instructions to the Observer: You will need to know a variety of possible techniques or types. Keep a tally of those you observe. At the end of the observation period, count the number of occurrences of each technique or type.

Techniques or Types: Grouping Patterns	Number of Occurrences
Homogeneous Grouping for Skills	10
Interest Grouping	7
Management Grouping	5
Groups Based on Book Read	3
Groups for Completing Project	2
Total # of Groups Used Week of November 4, 19—	27

To gain additional insight into the grouping patterns used in Mrs. Menotti's classroom, the percentage of times particular types of grouping patterns were used might be interesting. For example, 37 percent of the groups in Mrs. Menotti's classroom were homogenous skill groups, and 26 percent were based on interest.

Coding Systems

Another simple, structured tool for observing in classrooms is a coding system. A coding system looks for specific elements of teacher and/or student behavior. The observer usually records these elements at specific intervals, or simply tallies the number of times the particular behavior occurs. To complete a coding observation, an observer needs a list of specified behaviors. In this chapter we will provide three examples of coding systems: two based on Ned Flanders's student and teacher interaction system and one based on Norris Sanders's system of questioning.

In the first type of coding, the observer records the interaction during specific intervals.

Observing Student-Teacher Interaction

In each of the teacher-student interaction examples, the observer tallies the number of times the following nine categories of interaction between the teacher and students occur.

The first four types of interaction, according to Flanders, show an **indirect teacher influence:**

(1). **Accepts feelings**—The teacher accepts or acknowledges student-expressed feelings/concerns in a non-threatening manner. (For example, *Student:* "I don't understand the assignment." *Teacher:* "It is a difficult concept to grasp, isn't it?")

(2). **Praises and encourages**—The teacher gives positive evaluation of a student contribution. (For example, *Teacher:* "That's an especially good paper, Sammy.")

(3). **Accepts or uses ideas of student**—The teacher clarifies, develops or refers to a student contribution, usually without evaluation. (For example, *Student:* "The electoral college decides which presidential candidate is elected." *Teacher:* "And, the electoral college awards its votes based on the popular vote in each state.")

(4). **Asks questions**—The teacher solicits information or asks opinions with the intent that a student answer. (For example, *Teacher:* "What is one fact about the electoral college?")

The next three types of teacher-student interaction are considered to be **direct teacher influences:**

(5). **Lectures**—The teacher presents ideas, information, or orientation. Lecturing includes rhetorical questions.

(6). **Gives directions**—The teacher directs or suggests in a way which indicates that the student is expected to comply. (For example, *Teacher:* "Turn to page 72 and complete exercise 'B.' ")

(7). **Criticizes or justifies authority**—The teacher evaluates a student's contribution negatively or refers to the teacher's authoritative position. (For example, *Teacher:* "No, George, the electoral college is not a college for engineers. Where are the notes you took yesterday on this? You know it is your responsibility to take notes in class every day.")

The following two responses fall under the heading of **student talk:**

(8). **Student talk-response**—The student directly answers the teacher's question. The answer is usually responsive to the question. (For example, *Teacher:* "What is one fact about the electoral college?" *Student:* "The electoral college decides which presidential candidate is elected.")

(9). **Student talk-initiation**—The student initiates a comment or question that is unpredictable and/or creative in content. (For example, *Student:* "We didn't discuss this yesterday, but I know that eleven presidents have won the election by winning in electoral college votes but losing the popular vote.")

SAMPLE FORM 6

CODING SYSTEM FORM I—STUDENT-TEACHER INTERACTION DURING SPECIFIED INTERVALS

Name of Observer: Karen Susan Richie

Date and Time of Observation: February 5, 19— 10:30 a.m.

Length of Observation: 30 minutes

Intervals at Which Behavior Is Recorded: Every two minutes

Element Observed: Student-Teacher Interaction

Teacher and/or Student: Mrs. Menotti

Grade Level and/or Subject: Second grade

Objective of Observation: To examine student-teacher interaction

Instructions to the Observer: After each interval, record the instance you have observed. Identify the people whose behavior you are observing, and specifically describe their behavior. If possible, use direct quotes. Finally, indicate the code number of the instance you have observed from the codes listed on pages 9 and 10.

Name	Behavior	Code
Joey	to Mrs. M.: "Mrs. M., I finished my book and I need to see if I can find it in the library."	9
Mrs. M.	to Joey: "Is it in the classroom library, Joey?"	4
Joey	to Mrs. M.: "Yes."	8
Mrs. M.	to Joey: "O.K., you can look for it, Joey. Just don't disturb the rest of us while you're looking."	1,6
Mrs. M.	to Joey: "Have you found it?"	4
Joey	to Mrs. M.: "Not yet."	8
Mrs. M.	to Joey: "Well, join us while I read, and you can go back to the library and look afterward."	1,6
Mrs. M.	to Sandy: "Can you remember what happened to the rabbit when the boy got sick?"	4
Sandy	to Mrs. M.: "They took him from the nursery."	8
Maggie	to group: "They were afraid the rabbit was comintated [sic]."	8,9
Mrs. M.	to Maggie: "Do you mean contaminated?"	4
Maggie	to Mrs. M.: "Yes."	8

Mrs. M.	to Maggie: "Very good, Maggie. That's right."	2
Mrs. M.	to Sean: "Why do you think they were afraid the rabbit might be contaminated, Sean?"	3
Sean	to Mrs. M.: "Well, he was stuffed and the boy is real sick, so the rabbit might have germs."	8
Mrs. M.	to Sean: "Very good, Sean."	2

A second way to conduct a coding observation based on Flanders's modified interaction analysis is to total the number of times particular behaviors occur during a specified period of time, and to determine the percentage of time each behavior was observed, based on the total number of interactive behaviors during the observation period.

SAMPLE FORM 7

CODING SYSTEM FORM II—TYPE AND TALLY OF STUDENT-TEACHER INTERACTION

Name of Observer: Eric Dreibholz

Date and Time of Observation: December 16, 19— 2:15 p.m.

Length of Observation: 1 hour

Element Observed: Teacher-Student interaction

Teacher and/or Student: Mrs. Rodriguez

Grade Level and/or Subject: Sixth grade - Social Studies (Civil War)

Objective of Observation: To examine types of indirect and direct teacher interaction with students and type of student talk in one lesson

Instructions to the Observer: Tally the number of times each interactive behavior occurs during your observation period. Try to record at least one example of each type of interaction. At the end of the observation period, total the number of all teacher-student interactions and calculate the percentage of the total for each interaction.

Type of Interactive Behavior	Tally of Times Observed	Percentage
INDIRECT		
Accepts Feelings: Example: "I know some of you don't feel well. You may be discouraged but let's keep trying."	̶H̶H̶	8%
Praises/Encourages: Example: "I like what you're saying." "Good." "Can you tell us more?"	̶H̶H̶ ///	12%

Accepts or Uses Student Ideas:	////	7%
Example: "Nick said General Lee was an outstanding leader—let's talk about that."		
Asks Questions:	++++ ++++ ///	21%
Example: "Why do you think General Lee surrendered at that time?" "What was the turning point of the war?"		
DIRECT		
Lectures:	///	5%
Example: Gave background of Gettysburg Address		
Gives Directions:	++++ //	11%
Example: "Think about this question." "Answer questions 1–6 on p. 97."		
Criticizes or Justifies Authority:	///	5%
Example: "I don't like the way you crumbled your paper."		
STUDENT TALK		
Student Talk-Response:	++++ ++++ ///	21%
Example: Students answered all directed questions one/two words/deeper explanations		
Student Talk-Initiation:	++++ /	10%
Example: "I agree with Tom, but I think Lee should have waited longer before he surrendered."		
TOTALS	62	100%

The type of interaction most frequently used: Accepts or uses student ideas and student talk-response.

Adapted from Ned Flanders, 1985.

Observing Questioning Techniques

There are many approaches for examining questions asked by teachers. A coding system can help observers examine the types of questions asked. We will focus on a technique developed by Norris Sanders, (see table 1.1) based on the cognitive taxonomy of Benjamin Bloom. Bloom's cognitive taxonomy assumes that development of cognitive ability is hierarchical. In other words, understanding of concepts progresses from simple understanding, what Bloom calls knowledge or recall (Sanders calls this memory), and comprehension (Sanders calls this translation and interpretation) to more complex knowledge. Bloom labels these higher levels of cognition as analysis, synthesis, and evaluation. In between the less and more complex levels of understanding is the ability to apply (application) one's knowledge to problems and new situations. Bloom's cognitive taxonomy is diagramed in figure 1.1. As the chart shows, knowledge is cyclical. Once high levels of knowledge of a concept are achieved, an individual must begin to add to this knowledge by developing new concepts.

Sanders, using Bloom's taxonomy, identifies seven levels of questions, from least to most complex.

1. *Memory:* The student recalls or recognizes information.
2. *Translation:* The student changes information into a different symbolic form or language.
3. *Interpretation:* The student discovers relationships among facts, generalizations, definitions, values, and skills.
4. *Application:* The student solves a real-life problem that requires identification of the issue and the selection and use of appropriate generalizations and skills.
5. *Analysis:* The student solves a problem in the light of conscious knowledge of the parts and forms of thinking.
6. *Synthesis:* The student solves a problem that requires original, creative thinking.
7. *Evaluation:* The student makes a judgment of good or bad, right or wrong, according to standards he designates. (Sanders 1966, p. 3)

If you compare Sanders's levels of questions to Bloom's taxonomy, you will note a few minor differences. Sanders calls the lowest level of questioning *memory* rather than *recall,* as it is designated by Bloom. And Sanders divides the second level of the domain, *comprehension,* into two levels of questions: *translation* and *interpretation.*

To recognize the level of question asked, the observer must be able to examine the question and place it at the appropriate level. The best way to do this is to list all questions asked by the teacher, oral and written, and examine them based on examples of each level provided in table 1.1. The observer can also use the verbs provided in the central circle of Bloom's cognitive domain in figure 1.1 to identify the level of a question. The use of a cassette recorder is very helpful in this process. The student observer is cautioned simply to list or record the questions without attempting the examination process until each question asked can be carefully compared with sample questions. It is important to note that if two observers listen to the same lesson, it is likely that even if the questions are identically recorded, the observers' placement of them within levels will differ to some extent.

Since most educators, including Bloom and Sanders, agree that too many lower-level questions (memory, translation, interpretation), and not enough higher-level questions (application, analysis, synthesis, evaluation) are asked, it is helpful to note the frequency of the type of question asked. Observers should keep in mind, however, that in a well-planned lesson, the level of questions asked will directly relate to the teacher's objective for the students. For example, if the teacher's objective is, "The students will examine the feud in *Romeo and Juliet,*" it is likely that the questions asked will be at the lower levels. If however, the objective is, "The students will compare and contrast the feud in *Romeo and Juliet* with other literary and non-literary feuds," the questions will move from memory to analysis.

FIGURE 1.1

Cognitive Behaviors and Verbs* Based on Bloom's Cognitive Domain

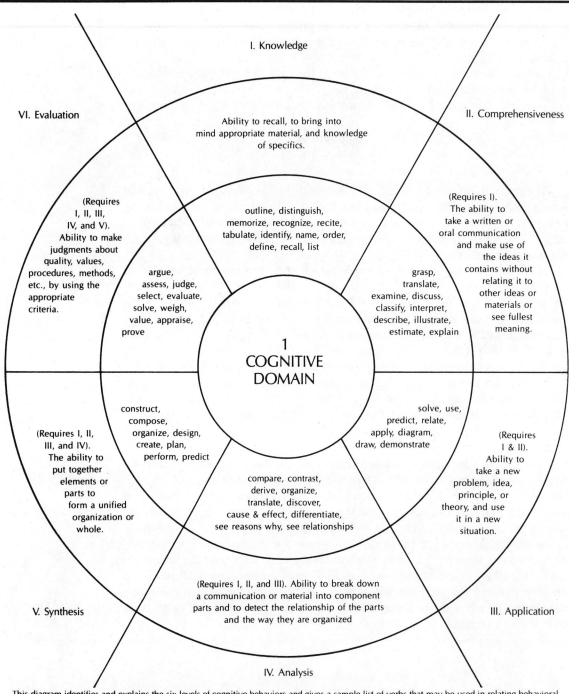

This diagram identifies and explains the six levels of cognitive behaviors and gives a sample list of verbs that may be used in relating behavioral objective evaluation to the proper level of cognitive behavior.

*Adapted by Sanchon S. Funk, Jeffrey L. Hoffman, Anne Keithley, and Bruce E. Long of the Florida State University Office of Field Experiences from Benjamin Bloom et. al. (ed.), *Taxonomy of Educational Objectives: Cognitive Domain*, Longmans, Green, and Company, Inc., 1985.

TABLE 1.1

Examples of Levels of Questions Based on Sanders and Bloom

---

1. Memory

How much is . . . .
Who is . . . .
What was . . . .
When was . . . .
Outline the chapter.

2. Translation

What does the definition say?
What is the English translation of that passage?
Look on page 27; what does your text say about . . . .
Draw a picture of the character in the story we read.

3. Interpretation

In your own words, what does that passage mean?
Without looking at your text, what is meant by . . . .
Write a sentence using the vocabulary word . . . .
Explain the meaning of the graph.
What is the word problem asking you to do?
Estimate the number of votes needed to win?

4. Application

What would happen if . . . .
What would you do in a similar situation?
How would you solve that problem?
Using this play as a model, write your own play based on the story we read.
Solve the word problem.
Diagram the . . . .
Demonstrate . . . .

5. Analysis

Compare this story to that story.
Contrast this battle to that battle.
What was the effect of his decision?
What caused the problem?
Is this story based on fact or opinion?
What is the major theme of the novel?
What conclusion would you derive from the following . . . .

6. Synthesis

Write an essay about . . . .
Write an original short story.
Design your own experiment.
Using all you have learned about oil painting and portraiture, paint a portrait in oils.
Develop solutions for the problem of . . . .
Write a computer program.

7. Evaluation

Write a critique of the novel . . . .
Evaluate the quality of . . . .
Argue the following point . . . .
Debate . . . .
Write a point-counterpoint paper on . . . .
Based on all you have learned, evaluate your own work.
Whose solution proved the most effective?

SAMPLE FORM 8

OBSERVATION FORM FOR
EXAMINING QUESTIONS

Name of Observer: <u>Ramon Auenida</u>

Date and Time of Observation: <u>December 11, 19— 1:15 p.m.</u>

Teacher: <u>Mr. Cortines</u>

Grade Level and/or Subject: <u>Tenth grade, science—"The Characteristics of Life"</u>

Objective of Observation: <u>To examine the level of questions asked by Mr. Cortines</u>

Instructions to the Observer: On a separate piece of paper or on a cassette record all questions asked by the teacher, orally and in writing, for one lesson. Then place each question below at the appropriate level. Next, tally the number of questions at each level. Count the total number of questions asked, and compute a percentage for each level.

1. Memory:
—What is another name for a living thing?
—What are the characteristics common to all living things?
—How do living things obtain food?
—What kind of energy do plants need in order to carry out photosynthesis?
—Who discovered the existence of micro-organisms?   Total # of Memory Questions: 5

2. Translation:
—Tell me in your own words what photosynthesis means.
—Explain the meaning of spontaneous generation.
—What is the derivation of metabolism?   Total # of Translation Questions: 3

3. Intepretation:
—How does movement in plants differ from movement in animals?
—What happens to energy taken into an organism?   Total # of Interpretation Questions: 2

4. Application:
—What would happen to the plants in this room if they didn't get sun and water?
—Diagram the concept of photosynthesis.   Total # of Application Questions: 2

5. Analysis:
—What are similarities and differences between living and nonliving things?
—Which of the scientist's experiments supported abiogenesis and which supported biogenesis?
—How does the movement of an animal differ from the movement of a windup toy?

Total # of Analysis Questions: 3

6. Synthesis:
—Write a paper on pasteurization. Discuss what the process is, how it is done, and why it is done.
—Do an oral report on how people do home canning from things that grow in their gardens. Explain how these procedures relate to the experiments on spontaneous generation described in this chapter.   Total # of Synthesis Questions: 2

7. Evaluation:
—Whose experiments do you think were most effective—Spallanzani's, Needham's or Pasteur's? Why?   Total # of Evaluation Questions: 1

Total # of Questions, All Levels: 18

Percentage of Memory 27%; Translation 17%; Interpretation 11%; Application 11%; Analysis 17%; Synthesis 11%; Evaluation 6%.

Checklists

A checklist is a simple structured tool to use while observing in a classroom. It serves the function of limiting the observation to the items on the list and allows the observer simply to mark when a task has been completed. The checklist does not evaluate; it documents.

Although many commercial checklists are available, the best checklists are specifically designed for the observation at hand. As with all observational tools, it is essential that the observer limit the items on the checklist to the objectives set for the specific observation. The keys to developing a good checklist are: (1) knowing the purpose for the checklist and (2) developing items that help the observer determine whether the items looked for are found. Checklists can be designed to look for many things in the classroom, such as the classroom environment, classroom management techniques, elements of the curriculum, teaching behaviors, and competencies taught. We have provided one checklist for observing classroom management.

SAMPLE FORM 9

CHECKLIST FOR AUTHORITARIAN MANAGEMENT MODEL

Name of Observer: <u>Alicia Wilkinson</u>

Date and Time of Observation: <u>November 25, 19— 11:15 a.m.</u>

Length of Observation: <u>Approximately 40 minutes</u>

Teacher: <u>Mrs. Sanderson</u>

Grade Level and/or Subject: <u>Third grade</u>

Objective of Observation: <u>To examine elements of authoritarian management in a classroom</u>

Instructions to the Observer: Prior to the observation, read over the items on the authoritarian management model checklist. These represent the elements that should be present in classrooms in which authoritarian management is used. During and after the observation, place a check next to those elements you have observed.

- ✓ Students understand the teacher's expectations and act accordingly.
- ___ Students exhibit productive work and study behaviors.
- ✓ Students understand and adhere to school and classroom rules.
- ___ Students evidence feelings of self-worth.
- ___ Students feel free to express themselves to the teacher and to one another.
- ✓ Students follow clearly established routines.
- ___ Students show respect for persons and property.
- ___ Students communicate openly and honestly.
- ___ Students manifest positive interpersonal relationships.
- ___ Students feel accountable for their own behavior.
- ___ Students exhibit group cohesiveness.
- ✓ Students understand and accept the consequences of their actions.
- ___ Students feel that they are treated fairly.
- ___ Students exhibit cooperativeness and a sharing attitude.
- ___ Students display productive group norms.
- ✓ Students quickly return to task after interruptions.
- ✓ Students follow directions.
- ✓ Students are prepared for the task at hand.
- ✓ Students function at a noise level appropriate to the activity.
- ✓ Students participate actively in learning tasks.
- ___ Students display positive feelings about classroom processes.
- ___ Students manifest the ability to adjust to changing situations.
- ___ Students exhibit self-discipline and self-control.
- ___ Students feel comfortable and safe.
- ___ Students display initiative and creativity.

_____ Students serve as resources to one another.

✓ Students move from one task to another in an orderly manner.

_____ Students accept and respect authority.

_____ Students support and encourage one another.

_____ Students are responsible for individual supplies and materials.

✓ Students pay attention to the teacher and to one another.

_____ Students like being members of the classroom group.

_____ Students feel that the teacher understands them.

_____ Students believe that they have opportunities to be successful.

Checklist items based on the work of Wilford A. Weber, *Classroom Management*, 1982, pp. 289–290.

Structured Observation of a Lesson

One way to observe the structure of a lesson is to use a lesson-planning form on which elements of a lesson are outlined. The observer can watch a lesson being taught and outline the lesson using specific examples on the lesson-planning form. Of course, it is important to note that not all lessons have all the elements of a particular structure. And each element may be included in more than one lesson. Sometimes lessons include elements in a variety of orders. At times, only a few of the elements occur. We have chosen to provide an example based on the work of Madeline Hunter and developed by Lois Sprinthall. However, any lesson-planning form can be used.

SAMPLE FORM 10

FORM FOR STRUCTURED OBSERVATION OF A LESSON

Name of Observer: <u>Angie Carl</u>

Date and Time of Observation: <u>November 11, 19— 12:40 p.m.</u>

Teacher: <u>Olivia Smith</u>

Grade Level and/or Subject: <u>Seventh grade; Social Studies; Civil War</u>

Objective of Observation: <u>To identify how the elements of a lesson are implemented by the teacher</u>

Instructions to the Observer: As you observe in the classroom, list the elements of the lesson under the categories below. A description of each category appears in italics.

(1) **Anticipatory Set -** *In every lesson the teacher provides initial motivation and focus for the lesson. Sometimes this focus takes the form of a review of previous knowledge important to this lesson; at other times it is designed to "grab" the students' attention. Key words: alerting, relevance, relationship (to previous lesson), meaningfulness, etc.*

Teacher reads from letters by two brothers, one fighting for the North, the other for the South. Students are attentive and appear to be listening.

(2) **Objective** - *In almost every lesson the teacher specifies the behaviors the students will be expected to perform. In other words, the student knows what is expected of him/her and what s/he is expected to learn.*

Objective on board is pointed out to the students—"The student will compose a letter from the perspective of a soldier from the North or the South during the Civil War."

(3) **Teacher Input** - *In most lessons the teacher will provide the student with the information needed to reach the objective successfully. Sometimes the teacher will show the student how to accomplish the task by modeling appropriate performance.*

Using a variety of questioning techniques, the students and the teacher review two battles discussed in previous lesson. Teacher lists key information on overhead projector.

The students are reminded to be sure they have all this information in their notebooks since they will need it to complete their assignment.

(4) **Checking for Understanding** - *Throughout the lesson the teacher checks to ensure that the students understand the concepts or skills being taught. This can be accomplished through random questioning or individual tutoring.*

The teacher asks the students if they understand the importance of these two battles. She then discusses with the students how the perspective of the Northern and Southern soldiers would have differed in each battle.

As the students work together, the teacher circulates to be sure they are on task and understanding what they are to do.

(5) **Guided Practice** - *In every lesson the student practices the expected performance. This may include exercises completed with the teacher, examples done by students on the board, students reading aloud, students working together to complete assignments, games that allow the students to exhibit understanding, etc.*

The teacher brainstorms with the students a Southern soldier's impression of one of the two battles. The brainstorming is listed on the board—the information about the battle is still projected on the screen above the board.

The teacher tells the students to do the same in small groups from the perspective of a Northern soldier in the same battle.

The teacher and the students compose one letter from a Northern soldier to his sweetheart on the overhead.

(6) **Independent Practice** - *The student independently exhibits the behaviors set forth in the objective. To accomplish this, the student might complete problems, write a paper, do an experiment, give a report, complete a project, do research, etc.*

The students are instructed to begin a letter from either a Northern or Southern soldier to a member of his family or friend from the other battle. They are told to use the same process—first brainstorming with him/herself about what that soldier is feeling, and then writing the letter.

(7) **Closure** - *The teacher helps the student review what s/he has learned in the lesson. This may include a summary of the lesson, questions about what happened during the student's independent practice, the students' report of their progress, an evaluation by the teacher, relationship of this lesson to the next lesson or the unit, assignment of additional independent practice.*

The teacher asks for a Northern and Southern volunteer to tell the class what s/he has written or brainstormed thus far.

From: Lois Sprinthall, *A Strategy Guide for Teachers: Guide Book for Supervisors of Novice Teachers.* Unpublished manuscript.

Interview Methods

Frequently, observations do not yield enough data for complete understanding of the situation. For example, it is not always possible to observe all the grouping patterns employed in a single classroom over a period of weeks. University students are unlikely to be able to return two weeks after an initial classroom observation to observe other classes of the same teacher. Therefore, observers are unable to see how the grouping patterns change and develop based on the students and the content. An interview with the teacher, when conducted objectively, can help the observer determine this sequence. The interview should be designed to reveal data that cannot be observed in one observation, or even in a series.

The interview is a fact-finding technique in which an attempt is made to obtain information from the respondent through direct questioning. Of course, a good interview requires planning and nonjudgmental questions that reveal important data.

Below is a checklist of important interviewing techniques to use prior to and during an interview.

SAMPLE FORM 11

CHECKLIST OF INTERVIEWING TECHNIQUES

Name of Observer: <u>Maria Ortiz</u>

Date and Time of Observation: <u>November 6, 19—, Teacher's Classroom,</u>
<u>3:30 p.m.</u>

Person to Be Interviewed: <u>Mr. Maldonado</u>

Grade Level and/or Subject: <u>Fifth grade</u>

Objective of Observation: <u>To find out about different grouping patterns than those</u>
<u>observed on November 4, 19—</u>

Instructions to the Observer: Review this checklist prior to and after your interview. Check off items you have completed.

Prior to the Interview

✔ Establish a purpose of the interview.

✔ Request an appointment (time and place) giving sufficient lead time for you and the person to be interviewed.

✔ Plan objective, specific questions related to the purpose of the interview.

✔ Prioritize questions, asking the most important first.

✔ Remind the person to be interviewed of the time, place, and purpose of the interview.

The Interview

✔ Arrive at preestablished place several minutes before the scheduled time for the interview.

✔ Start the interview by reminding the person to be interviewed of the purpose of the interview.

✔ Request permission to tape the interview (if appropriate).

✔ If unable to tape, take careful, objective notes trying to list direct quotes as often as possible.

✔ Avoid inserting impressions or judgments.

✔ Limit the interview to no more than 15–30 minutes.

After the Interview

✔ Review with the respondent what has been said or heard.

✔ Express your appreciation for the interview.

✔ Offer to share the interview report with the respondent.

2

OBSERVING CLASSROOMS, SCHOOLS, AND CURRICULUM

ANECDOTAL OBSERVATION OF CLASSROOMS, SCHOOLS, AND CURRICULUM

Anecdotal observations can be completed while observing the classroom, the school, and the curriculum. These observations can reveal many interesting aspects of the operation of the school and its instructional program and how individual teachers adapt the instructional program to their students. In addition, these observations can show how teachers and schools deal with physical constraints such as overcrowding, lack of equipment, and poor facilities.

Anecdotal Observations of Classrooms

An anecdotal observation of classroom organization includes a description of the physical environment and its layout. It is important to include information about the lighting source and whatever classroom decoration is displayed.

23

SAMPLE FORM 12

FORM FOR ANECDOTAL RECORD
OF CLASSROOM ORGANIZATION

Name of Observer: Marvin Anderson

Date and Time of Observation: September 19, 19— 8:15 a.m.

Length of Observation: 30 minutes

Person and/or Event Observed: Mr. Schroeder's classroom

Grade Level and/or Subject: Fourth grade; all subjects

Objective of Observation: To see how Mr. Schroeder's classroom is organized

Instructions to the Observer: As completely and accurately as possible, describe the organization of the classroom. Be sure to include as much detail as possible. Try to avoid making judgments.

The classroom is quite small for the 29 students. The students' desks are arranged in five rows of five or six desks each, with the chalkboard in the front. The desks have small cubbies in them and separate chairs. In the front of the room to the students' right is a stool and a small podium. To the students' left are windows that run the length of the room. The shades are pulled against the morning sun. On the students' right are high windows that are on the hallway; beneath these windows are bulletin boards. Mr. Schroeder's desk is at the rear of the classroom next to the exterior windows. Next to the window is a four-drawer file cabinet. On the other side of the teacher's desk is a student desk and chair. At the right rear is a student worktable and eight chairs. Behind the worktable, along most of the rear wall, are student cubbies and bookshelves. On the floor there is a royal blue carpet that has many stains on it.

Light in the classroom is good. There is a lot of exterior light from outside and additional light from the hallway. The classroom is additionally lit by long fluorescent fixtures. Mr. Schroeder has a lamp on his desk which is also lit. Under the exterior windows is a ledge. Under about one quarter of the length of the ledge is the heating and cooling unit. The classroom is air-conditioned. Under the rest there are bookcases and cabinets.

Above the front chalkboard is a bulletin board. On this board is a large poster with the classroom rules. Also on this bulletin board there are some mass-produced posters about the writing process and reading books. Near the center of this bulletin board there is a group of a dozen or so hanging maps. On the bulletin boards to the students' right there is an opening school display with all the students' photographs. Under each photo is a paper that the student wrote on the first day of school, introducing himself or herself to Mr. Schroeder. The next bulletin board is empty. Nearest the door to the hallway at the rear right are school announcements and the weekly list of classroom jobs. The jobs include plants, attendance, lunch monitor, hallway monitor, bus monitor, playground monitors, classroom monitors, and care of pets. The names of one or more students are listed next to each job. Along the top of the cubbies at the rear of the room there are plants. Next to the cubbies there is a watering can with a long spout. On top of one of the bookshelves there is an aquarium; nearby is a cage with two gerbils (I think).

Along the ledge under the exterior windows are what appear to be learning centers. Most seem to be related to the Revolutionary War. One deals with the battles of the Revolution; another with the personalities of the war. I can't read the headings on the other two. Nearest the front of the room on the ledge there is a globe.

When the students enter the room it is very crowded. There is not much room between their desks, and they are continuously bumping into one another. It gets noisy very quickly. Mr. Schroeder is in the front of the room with the attendance monitor for the week, taking attendance and collecting lunch money. Several students are milling around the podium trying to ask the teacher questions. Three boys are sitting at the table at the rear of the room. Mr. Schroeder walks up to them to tell them that they will have new desks for them by the end of the week, though he's not quite sure where they'll put them. The students on the left side of the room are so close to the ledge that it would not be possible to use the learning centers without moving their desks. (I'll watch to see how Mr. Schroeder handles this later.) A girl raises her hand and asks if she can go to the restroom to get water for the gerbils. Mr. Schroeder says, "Take the restroom pass and the watering can and also get enough water for the plants." She leaves.

The intercom clicks on and Mr. Schroeder attempts to "shush" the talking students. They get quieter, but continue to talk. He walks to the rear of the room and flicks the lights; most of the students quiet down. However, the boys at the rear table are still talking. He walks over to them, and points to the classroom rules, one of which is "respect others when they are speaking." They quiet down. When the announcements are over, Mr. Schroeder has each of the three boys go to a chart under the class rules and put a check next to his name. If the students get five checks during the week, they cannot participate in Fun Friday, which is an event that occurs each Friday afternoon.

Another method of classroom observation is to draw a simple diagram of the classroom to illustrate the seating arrangement and the placement of other furniture and equipment. Since a diagram cannot show what is on the bulletin boards or walls, the observer should discuss these elements after mapping the classroom.

SAMPLE FORM 13

FORM FOR A CLASSROOM MAP

Name of Observer: Shannon Anthony

Date and Time of Observation: September 16, 19—

Person and/or Event Observed: Mrs. Romano

Grade Level and/or Subject: Fourth grade

Objective of Observation: To determine how the organization of the classroom relates to the instruction, management, and motivation of students

Instructions to the Observer: Draw a map of the classroom you are observing. Include seating arrangements, placement of furniture and other equipment. Then give a brief anecdotal description of these elements of the classroom: lighting, traffic patterns, instructional displays, management, and motivational elements.

Draw classroom map:

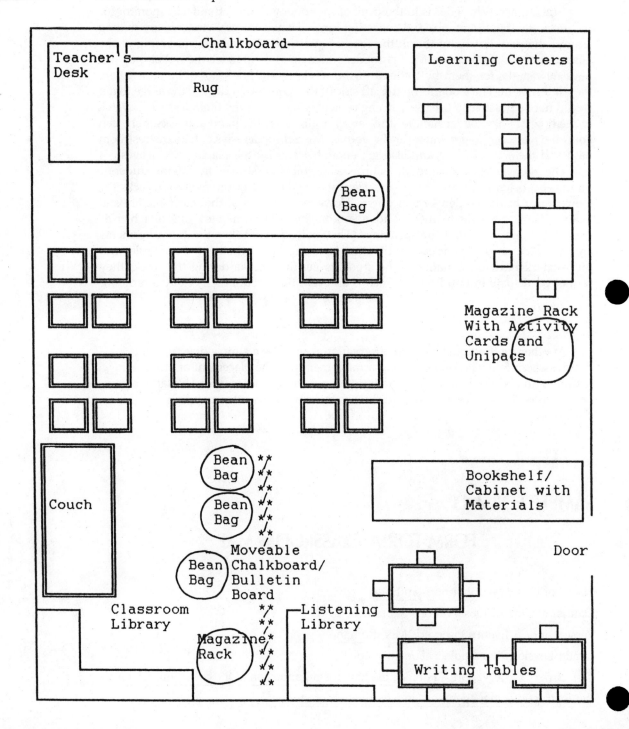

Anecdotal discussion of classroom elements:

Lighting and Traffic Patterns: Classroom is bright with windows along the length of one of the long walls. In addition the classroom has a skylight over the library area. Although the classroom is very full, the traffic flows fairly well. The only exception is when all students must move from their desks at the same time. However, this is not a frequent occurrence, since the children sit at their desks rarely.

Instructional Displays, Management and Motivational Elements: There are numerous displays on bulletin boards across the wall opposite the window wall. In addition, student books are displayed in the class library and on the wall above the writing tables. The movable chalkboard and bulletin board also serve to display student work. Student-made mobiles hang from the ceiling and other student art work is in the hallway immediately outside of the classroom serving as a motivation. The displays are colorful and all students have some work displayed. On one of the bulletin boards is a list of student jobs that include: watering plants, shelving books in the library, filing cassettes in the listening library, cleaning the chalkboards, organizing the bookshelf and materials cabinet, helping the aide change the bulletin boards, vacuuming the rug, and cleaning the floors. It is clear that students are expected to maintain the classroom.

Many other anecdotal observations of the classroom can be useful. For example, observers may focus on the instructional elements of the classroom or on how the students move throughout the classroom for a variety of purposes. Marvin notes in his anecdotal discussion of Mr. Schroeder's classroom that it is crowded and that three of the students do not yet have their own desks. Marvin may want to spend part of a day observing how Mr. Schroeder deals with this problem. If the students are using the learning centers during social studies, what happens to the student desks nearest the ledge? Does Mr. Schroeder use the rear table for reading or other groups? What happens to the three boys if they are not a part of the group using the table? When students leave the classroom for special classes, how do they do so without disturbing the other students?

Anecdotal Observations of Schools

Similar anecdotal observations can be done on various aspects of an entire school. Observing students in hallways during a change of class periods can reveal a great deal about the organization of the school. It can also be interesting to examine the "decorations" in the hallways. Are there bulletin boards displaying student work? Do the bulletin boards have locked glass doors? Are there display cabinets in the hallways? What is in these cabinets? Are the hallways well lit? Do the students have individual lockers? Where are the various school administrative offices? Are they easily accessible to students, teachers, and visitors? How are the offices furnished? What are the "decorations" in the offices which cater to students, such as the guidance office? What are the school grounds like? How about the lunchroom, auditorium, and gym?

Are there public areas in which students gather? Where are they, and what are they like? What is the playground like? Is there playground equipment? Examining all these elements helps the observer get to know the school better.

Anecdotal Observations of Curriculum

Anecdotal observations can also be used to examine the curriculum. The observer in Mr. Schroeder's classroom might want to know more about the social studies curriculum. He might write an anecdotal observation that includes information about the text and other classroom materials. Or, he might discuss more detailed information about the learning centers. The observer might seek out the school, district, or state curriculum guide to see what is taught in fourth grade social studies. How does what Mr. Schroeder is teaching relate to what is required by the school, district, or state? The observer might compare Mr. Schroeder's interpretation of the curriculum in his lessons with the interpretation of another fourth grade teacher. These elements can all tell the observer a great deal about the school, its curriculum, and its instructional policies.

STRUCTURED OBSERVATION OF CLASSROOMS, SCHOOLS, AND CURRICULUM

Structured observations of classrooms, schools, and curriculum can be conducted by using the techniques of coding, checklists, interviews, and surveys. Structured observations allow the observer to look for very specific elements. Instruments may be developed by the observer, adapted from other sources, or copied from this text.

Observing the Social Environment in a Classroom

There are numerous ways to look at the social environment in a classroom. We will discuss one which is based on the research of Talcott Parsons and Edward A. Shills (1951) and Herbert J. Walberg and Gary J. Anderson (1968). This research has led to the development by Anderson (1973) of fifteen dimensions of a classroom social environment. These dimensions, with brief descriptions developed by Gary D. Borich (1990), are:

1. *Cohesiveness*—When a group of individuals interacts for a period of time, a feeling of intimacy or togetherness develops. Too much cohesiveness within a classroom may separate members of the group from nonmembers, and reduce the motivation and willingness of some students to become engaged in the learning process. Too little cohesiveness may discourage students from an allegiance to group norms, and encourage them to focus exclusively on their own personal interests and desires.

2. *Diversity*—The extent to which the class provides for different student interests and activities is important to school learning. Too much diversity in a classroom can make teaching to the average student difficult, while too little may fail to respond to individual learning needs.

3. *Formality*—The extent to which behavior within a class is guided by formal rules can influence the flexibility both teacher and students may need to achieve stated goals. A classroom with an extensive or inflexible system of rules and procedures might be less productive than a classroom with fewer rules that are phased in and out or changed periodically to accommodate changing goals and conditions.

4. *Speed*—Student commitment to the goals of the class is best achieved when students feel they are learning at the same rate as other students. Too fast a pace will discourage a commitment to group goals for less able learners, while too slow a pace will discourage a commitment from more able learners.

5. *Environment*—The classroom physical environment, including the amount of space and type of equipment, can influence the structure of the group and relationships among its members. Generally, the more the classroom reflects the world outside, the more opportunity there is to learn from the classroom environment.

6. *Friction*—This refers to the extent to which certain students are responsible for class tension and hostility among members of the class. The greater the friction, the more time spent on classroom management and the less the classroom is task-oriented.

7. *Goal direction*—Clearly stated goals and their acceptance by the group orient the class and provide expected roles for class members. Students in highly goal-directed classes are expected to reach instructional goals more quickly than students in classes where the goals are unspecified.

8. *Favoritism*—This indicates the extent to which some students and the teacher behave in ways that benefit some at the expense of others. A classroom in which there are many "favorites" lessens the self-concepts of those who are not, and disengages them from a commitment to class goals.

9. *Cliquishness*—Cliques within a class can lead to hostility among class members and alternate norms, which may lead to less optimal group productivity. A high degree of cliquishness can make some students become distracted or off-task, especially during group work, when students may be loyal to the clique and not obedient to the teacher.

10. *Satisfaction*—Whether or not students gain a sense of accomplishment from completing the events and activities that are assigned affects their learning. Low satisfaction or sense of accomplishment leads to greater frustration and less interest in the class, eventually reducing a student's need to achieve.

11. *Disorganization*—Class disorganization is believed to be related to reduced instructional time and, therefore, reduced opportunity to learn. Extreme disorganization can result in classroom management problems and large increases in the time needed to achieve instructional goals.

12. *Difficulty*—Generally, students who perceive the content as easy tend to perform more poorly on measures of achievement than those who do not. A high degree of perceived difficulty, however, will make some students give up and disengage from the learning task.

13. *Apathy*—Students who fail to see the purpose or relevance of class activities to themselves perform more poorly than those who do. These students fail to behave according to the accepted group norms, which increases the rate of misbehavior and time spent on classroom management.

14. *Democratic*—This indicates where the class perceives itself on the authoritarian-democratic continuum. Optimal learning may occur under both extremes, depending on the degree of warmth perceived by students. An authoritarian climate in which the teacher is warm and nurturing may be as productive for learning as a democratic climate in which students have greater control over their learning environment.

15. *Competitiveness*—The effect of competitiveness has been shown to differ widely both within and across classrooms. Too little or too much competitiveness is believed to be detrimental to learning, with repetitive cycles of competition and cooperation being optimal.

Based on these dimensions Borich developed a coding scale on which the observer indicates the level to which three elements of each dimension are observed in the classroom. An average score for each dimension on this scale, particularly when it is employed several times in the same classroom, can help observers become aware of various elements of a classroom's social environment. Borich points out that the scale is not appropriate for research purposes, but is particularly useful if observers complete several administrations of it while observing a variety of grouping patterns, across subject areas, over a long period of time.

SAMPLE FORM 14

FORM FOR CODING SCALE OF CLASSROOM SOCIAL ENVIRONMENT

Name of Observer: Enrique Valdez

Date and Time of Observation: January 15, 19— 10:40 a.m.

Length of Observation: 50 minutes

Person and/or Event Observed: Sara Schmidtson's classroom

Grade Level and/or Subject: First grade; mathematics

Objective of Observation: To observe the classroom social environment

Instructions to the Observer: Before using the scale, become familiar with the descriptions of each of the 15 dimensions of a classroom social environment. These descriptions will be found on pp. 28–30. The scale is divided into three sets (numbered 1–15, 16–30, and 31–45). Each item represents one element of one of the 15 dimensions. Every fifteenth item begins a new set of items, following the order of the dimensions in the first set (e.g., numbers 1, 16, and 31 represent one dimension; numbers 2, 17, and 32 another; and so on).

After observing in a classroom, mark the appropriate rating on each item. Note that some of the items are phrased negatively, and the numbers next to these items have been reversed. Average the three elements of each dimension (e.g., numbers 15, 30, and 45). Note that for several of the dimensions being measured (diversity, speed, difficulty, democracy, and competitiveness), a higher score is not necessarily more desirable.

	Strongly Disagree	Disagree	Agree	Strongly Agree	No Information
1. A student in this class has the chance to get to know all other students (cohesiveness).	1	2	3	④	N/I
2. The class has students with many different interests (diversity).	1	2	3	④	N/I
3. There is a set of rules for the students to follow (formality).	1	②	3	④	N/I
4. Most of the class has difficulty keeping up with the assigned work (speed).	1	②	3	4	N/I
5. The books and equipment students need or want are easily available in the classroom (environment).	1	2	3	④	N/I
6. There are tensions among certain students that tend to interfere with class activities (friction).	1	②	3	4	N/I
7. Most students have little idea of what the class is attempting to accomplish (goal direction).	④	3	2	1	N/I
8. The better students' questions are answered more sympathetically than those of the average student (favoritism).	1	2	③	4	N/I
9. Some students refuse to mix with the rest of the class (cliquishness).	1	2	③	4	N/I
10. The students seem to enjoy their classwork (satisfaction).	1	2	③	4	N/I
11. There are long periods during which the class does nothing (disorganization).	①	2	3	4	N/I
12. Some students in the class consider the work difficult (difficulty).	1	2	③	4	N/I
13. Most students seem to have a concern for the progress of the class (apathy).	4	③	2	1	N/I
14. When group discussions occur, all students tend to contribute (democracy).	1	②	3	4	N/I
15. Most students cooperate rather than compete with one another in this class (competitiveness).	4	3	②	1	N/I
16. Students in this class are not in close enough contact to develop likes and dislikes for one another.	4	③	2	1	N/I
17. The class is working toward many different goals.	1	②	3	④	N/I
18. Students who break the rules are penalized.	1	2	③	②	N/I
19. The class has plenty of time to cover the prescribed amount of work.	4	3	②	1	N/I
20. A comprehensive collection of reference material is available in the classroom for students to use.	1	②	3	4	N/I
21. Certain students seem to have no respect for other students.	1	2	③	4	N/I
22. The objectives of the class are not clearly recognized.	④	3	②	1	N/I
23. Every member of the class is given the same privileges.	4	3	②	1	N/I
24. Certain students work only with their close friends.	④	2	③	4	N/I
25. There is considerable student dissatisfaction with the classwork.	④	③	2	1	N/I
26. Classwork is frequently interrupted by some students with nothing to do.	4	③	2	1	N/I
27. Most students in this class are constantly challenged.	1	②	③	4	N/I
28. Some members of the class don't care what the class does.	1	2	③	④	N/I
29. Certain students have more influence on the class than others.	4	3	2	①	N/I
30. Most students in the class want their work to be better than their friends' work.	1	2	3	4	N/I
31. This class is made up of individuals who do not know each other well.	4	③	2	1	N/I
32. Different students are interested in different aspects of the class.	④	3	②	1	N/I
33. There is a right and wrong way of going about class activities.	④	3	②	1	N/I
34. There is little time in this class for daydreaming.	4	3	2	①	N/I
35. There are bulletin board displays and pictures around the room.	4	3	2	④	N/I
36. Certain students in this class are uncooperative.	1	2	3	④	N/I
37. Most of the class realizes exactly how much work is required.	1	2	3	④	N/I
38. Certain students in the class are favored over others.	①	2	3	4	N/I

39. Most students cooperate equally well with all class members.	4	3	2	①	N/I
40. After an assignment, most students have a sense of satisfaction.	1	2	3	④	N/I
41. The class is well organized and efficient.	4	3	2	①	N/I
42. Most students consider the subject matter easy.	4	3	②	1	N/I
43. Students show a common concern for the success of the class.	4	3	2	①	N/I
44. Each member of the class has as much influence as does any other member.	4	3	2	①	N/I
45. Students compete to see who can do the best work.	④	3	2	1	N/I

From: Gary Borich, *Observation Skills for Effective Teaching*, 1990, pp. 113–115.

A Study of the School and School Services

An excellent way to get to know how a school functions and what services it provides to students is to conduct interviews of school personnel using an interview checklist. The procedures for good interviews discussed in chapter 1, pp. 21–22, should be carefully followed.

SAMPLE FORM 15

CHECKLIST FOR SCHOOL PERSONNEL INTERVIEWS

Name of Interviewer: <u>Ramona Machung</u>

Instructions to Interviewer: Schedule a conference with an appropriate person from each administrative division of the school. If a specific service is not identified, discuss with the principal or assistant principal how the school provides the service to meet the needs of the students. Use the checklist to (1) formulate your questions and (2) ensure that you ask appropriate questions. You may add some of your own topics to the list. Check off each item for which you obtain an answer. Take notes in the space provided.

Guidance, Testing, Evaluation, and Reporting

Name of Person Interviewed: <u>Mr. Armstrong</u>

Title of Person Interviewed: <u>Guidance Counselor</u>

Date, Time, and Place of Interview: <u>December 3, 19—, 11:30 a.m., Mr. Armstrong's office</u>

Approximate Length of Interview: <u>15 minutes</u>

  ✔ 1. Purpose of guidance program
  ✔ 2. Procedures for obtaining services
  ✔ 3. Services of guidance program (individual and group)

✓ 4. Referral services
✓ 5. Services for pregnant students and single parents
✓ 6. Teachers' role in guidance
✓ 7. Students' role in guidance
✓ 8. Parents' role in guidance
✓ 9. Standardized tests and purpose
✓ 10. School's grading/reporting policies
✓ 11. School's promotion/retention policies
✓ 12. Academic advising and placing of students

Notes: Serves students, teachers, administrators, parents. Works with administrators and teachers on academic, psychological, and social placement and testing of students. Tests: Group and individual IQ tests, state competency tests, reading and Iowa Tests of Basic Skills. Individual students come for help with social/behavioral problems, help with scholarships, college selection. Helped develop sexuality education classes and set up daycare for single parents. Work with social workers, health of pregnant girls.

Library or Media Center/Instructional Materials and Equipment

Name of Person Interviewed: Mr. Andrade

Title of Person Interviewed: School Librarian/Media Specialist

Date, Time, and Place of Interview: December 6, 19—, 3:45 p.m., Library/Media Center

Approximate Length of Interview: 15 minutes

✓ 1. Available library materials related to subject and/or grade level
✓ 2. Library or media center hours for students and teachers
✓ 3. Procedures for using library or media center (class/students/teachers)
✓ 4. Vertical file and appropriate contents
✓ 5. Computer indexing of library materials
✓ 6. Equipment and media available for teachers' library/media center use
✓ 7. Checkout policies for students, teachers, and classes
✓ 8. Equipment and media available for classroom use
✓ 9. Procedures for instructing students in library/media center use
    10. Assistance available for use of equipment and media
✓ 11. Availability and procedures for computer use by students and teachers
    12. Procedures for selection and review of library materials and media

Notes: Explained where fiction, nonfiction, and reference materials were for all curricular areas for 6th grade. Library open 8:10–3:30 daily for students, 7:30–4:30 for teachers. Both computer and vertical file indexing. Equipment: 3 movie projectors, 6 overhead projectors, 5 slide projectors, 1 opaque projector. Checked out on a first come first serve basis, but for 35 minutes at a time. Seven computers for student use in small room off media center. Chart of instructions about computer indexing and library and computer use.

Health Services

Name of Person Interviewed: Mrs. Ginette Cortez

Title of Person Interviewed: Home-School Coordinator

Date, Time, and Place of Interview: December 13, 19—, 12:00 p.m., Health Clinic

Approximate Length of Interview: 20 minutes

- ✓ 1. Available health services at school
- ✓ 2. Services available through school referral
- ✓ 3. Sex education and condom distribution
- ✓ 4. Services for pregnant students
- ✓ 5. Procedures for teacher with ill/injured child
- ✓ 6. Procedures for dealing with HIV-positive student
- ✓ 7. School safety precautions, policies, and regulations
- ✓ 8. Other county/community services available to students
- ✓ 9. Health and related issues taught in classes

Notes: First aid, cot for resting—eye and ear exams at community clinics. Flu shots at county clinic, work with guidance counselors, teachers on sexuality education—no condoms distributed as yet but it has been discussed. School secretary calls parent/ caregiver when child is ill at school. When HIV positive, refer for second opinion, student can come to classes. No smoking/drugs, guns, pushing, running in halls, schoolgrounds allowed. Teach Diet, Nutrition, Exercise, sexuality education.

Curriculum Resource Person or Assistant Principal for Curriculum

Name of Person Interviewed: Mr. Roger Maldonado

Title of Person Interviewed: Assistant Principal

Date, Time, and Place of Interview: November 25, 19—, 9:15 a.m., Mr. Maldonado's office

Approximate Length of Interview: 30 minutes

- ✓ 1. School, district, county, or state curriculum guides
- ✓ 2. Multicultural aspects of the curriculum
- ✓ 3. School's organization for instruction:
     - ✓ a. grouping
     -     b. departmentalization
     - ✓ c. chain of command
     - ✓ d. curricular offerings
     - ✓ e. extra-curricular offerings
     - ✓ f. scheduling for teachers and students
- ✓ 4. Planning requirements for teachers
- ✓ 5. In-service and other opportunities for teachers
- ✓ 6. Observation and evaluation of teachers
- ✓ 7. Procedures for selection and review of textbooks and classroom materials
- ✓ 8. Teachers' role in curriculum development and implementation (may suggest ideas—not always implemented)

✔ 9. Community's role in curriculum development and implementation—None
✔ 10. Procedures for dealing with controversial issues and/or materials—None
✔ 11. Special education teachers
✔ 12. Reading teachers
✔ 13. Speech pathologists—None
✔ 14. Gifted program teachers
✔ 15. Social adjustment teachers, including drop-out prevention and in-school sus-pension—started 1990–1991 year—seems to be helping
✔ 16. Dean of boys/girls—yes
✔ 17. Music, art, and drama teachers—yes—once a week
✔ 18. Other special teachers (bilingual, physical education)
✔ 19. Procedures for mainstreaming students

Notes: Have county and state curriculum guides. Ability grouping for reading and mathematics, otherwise heterogeneous. Basic skills curriculum. Teachers plan week ahead, hand in plan books, planning time 30 min. daily. Principal observes new teachers 5 times a year; others 3 times—lets teachers know approximate days he will observe. Learning disability, reading, G.T. teachers. Students mainstreamed for music, art, social studies.

Person in Charge of Student Discipline

Name of Person Interviewed: Mr. Roger Maldonado

Title of Person Interviewed: Vice Principal

Date, Time, and Place of Interview: December 16, 19—, 3:40, Mr. Maldonado's office

Approximate Length of Interview: 15 minutes

✔ 1. Schoolpolicies/regulations regarding student behavior and appearance
✔ 2. Student handbook
✔ 3. Procedures for severe discipline referrals
✔ 4. Substance abuse programs
✔ 5. Drop-out prevention programs
✔ 6. School-administered discipline
✔ 7. Referrals to other agencies
✔ 8. Involvement of law enforcement in the school

Notes: Policies on drugs, guns, crime, smoking, all substance abuse in student and parent handbooks. Discipline rules in all classroms. Severe discipline problems referred to guidance counselor/principal/parent. Law officers can search lockers for suspected contents. When failing grades, placed in low student/teacher ratio—drop-out prevention programs. School does not use corporal punishment as of this year. Have individual group therapy meetings with guidance counselor.

Principal or Assistant Principal

Name of Person Interviewed: <u>Mrs. Elizabeth Andrews</u>

Title of Person Interviewed: <u>Principal</u>

Date, Time, and Place of Interview: <u>December 16, 19—, 4:30, Mrs. Andrew's office</u>

Approximate Length of Interview: <u>40 minutes</u>

   ✔ 1. School policies/regulations regarding teacher behavior and appearance.

   ✔ 2. Faculty handbook—<u>yes</u>

   ✔ 3. Faculty meetings (time and how used) <u>Weekly, 3:30 Discuss Parent's Day, Routines Curriculum-Testing</u>

   ✔ 4. Organizational pattern of local schools (i.e. board—central office—school)

   ✔ 5. Specialized type of school, such as magnet

   ✔ 6. Specialized programs, such as before-and after-school programs and preschool or childcare programs

   ✔ 7. Information about the community served by the school

   ✔ 8. Community and parent involvement in the school

   ✔ 9. Business involvement in the school

   ✔ 10. Professional organizations (i.e. union or academic)

   ✔ 11. Teachers' extra responsibilities

   ✔ 12. Student employment opportunities and procedures to follow

Notes: Appropriate, neat dress for males/females - may wear jeans, sweaters, sneakers. Teachers must sign in/out and be there from 7:30–4:15. There are 3 feeder elementary schools, 2 middle schools and 1 high school served by one county elected board of education. One elementary and county middle school are magnet schools. There is a before- and after-school program. Breakfast is served to low-income families. Day care provided for babies/young children of single teens. Teachers have bus, hall and lunch duties. Children cross town bussed in for integration but still 65 percent white, 35 percent minority. Attendance at PTAs varies—If children involved most parents come. If it is a decision about playground expansion, raising money—about half come. Parents do respond to notes, some help with homework. Local business gave 20 computers and 10 typewriters. Most teachers belong to a professional organization as well as NEA or AFT and state teacher's association. When ready to be certified, need to complete application at county office, provide resumé and make appointment with principal for an interview.

Examining the Teaching of Required Material

Most schools have a guide describing the required curriculum for each subject and the skills or competencies expected to be learned by the students. The guide may be produced at the school or school-district level and is usually based on state requirements. A checklist for examining which of these compe-tencies is actually performed in the classroom can be designed based on the objectives or content outline of any curriculum guide. For example, if you are observing in a seventh grade mathematics class as in the example below, you can design a checklist based on what the students are required to learn in mathematics, according to the curriculum guide. As you observe, you can check off those activities that actually are performed. Sample Form 16, a checklist based on competencies and performance indicators set by the North Carolina State Department of Public Instruction for seventh grade mathematics, is only partially listed below and is not filled in, since the method here is relatively simple and since each state will have its own curricular requirements. Form 16A will be found at the end of the book on p. 123. You should design your own checklist based on the curricular requirements in the school where you are observing.

SAMPLE FORM 16

CHECKLIST OF COMPETENCIES COVERED IN A 7TH GRADE MATH CLASSROOM

Name of Observer: _____

Date and Time of Observation: _____

Teacher: _____

School: _____

Instructions to the Observer: Using the list of competencies, goals, objectives, and/or performance indicators from a curriculum guide develop your own checklist. If the competency, goal, objective and/or performance indicator is observed, place an "X" in the right-hand column.

Goals, Objectives and/or Competencies	Performance Indicators	Observed
1. The learner will demonstrate an understanding of the decimal system of numeration	1.01 Read word names for whole numbers containing as many as seven digits 1.02 Read and write the numeral for any whole number less than ten million 1.03 Name the total value of a given digit of a whole number less than ten million 1.04 Round a whole number smaller than 10,000 to any designated place 1.05 Use <, =, or > to compare any two whole numbers	
2. The learner will compute with whole numbers	2.01 Estimate the sum of any three 4-digit numbers by rounding to the nearest 100 or 1,000 2.02 Add any three 4-digit numbers 2.03 Estimate to the nearest 100 or 1,000 the difference between two 4-digit numbers	

2.04 Subtract any two 4-digit numbers

2.05 Determine in a one-step problem-solving situation whether the information given is insufficient, sufficient, or extraneous

2.06 Translate a one-step problem-solving situation into an appropriate mathematical sentence

2.07 Estimate and then determine the solution of a problem-solving situation involving the addition or subtraction of up to 4-digit numbers

2.08 Estimate and then determine the product of a 3-digit number by a 2-digit number

2.09 Estimate and then determine the solution to a problem involving multiplication of a 3-digit by a 2-digit number

2.10 Estimate the quotient of a 4-digit number divided by a 2-digit number

2.11 Divide a 4-digit number by a 2-digit number

2.12 Divide a 3-digit number by a multiple of 10 less than 100

2.13 Raise a number to a given power

2.14 Express a product in its exponential form

2.15 Find the square root of a number by using a table of square roots or a calculator

2.16 Determine the factors of a whole number

2.17 Find the GCF (greatest common factor) of two whole numbers

2.18 Write a set of multiples of a whole number

2.19 Determine the LCM (least common multiple) of two whole numbers

2.20 Use the Commutative, Associative, and Distributive Properties for Addition and Multiplication to complete computations

2.21 Use zero in addition and one in multiplication as the Identity Elements for those operations

3. The learner will demonstrate an understanding of fractions and their applications

3.01 Read and write fractions

3.02 Change a fraction to its simplest form

3.03 Write a fraction equivalent to a given fraction

3.04 Change an improper fraction to either a mixed number or a whole number

3.05 Change a mixed number or a whole number into an improper fraction

3.06 Add two fractional numbers

3.07 Estimate the sum of two fractional numbers

3.08 Add two mixed numbers

3.09 Subtract two fractional numbers

3.10 Estimate the difference between two mixed numbers

3.11 Find the difference of two mixed numbers

3.12 Multiply two proper and/or improper fractional numbers

3.13 Determine the solution to a problem-solving situation involving the multiplication of fractional numbers

3.14 Determine the reciprocal of a fractional or mixed number

3.15 Find the quotient of two fractional numbers

3.16 Use $<$, $>$, or $=$ to compare two fractions

4. The learner will demonstrate an understanding of decimals and their applications	4.01 Read and write decimals through thousandths
	4.02 Read and write money (dollars and cents) through $1,000
	4.03 Use <, >, or = to compare two decimals
	4.04 Round a number less than 10 containing no more than two decimal places to the nearest whole number
	4.05 Estimate the sum of two or three decimal numbers

Adapted from: North Carolina Department of Public Instruction, Raleigh, N.C., *Competency Goals and Performance Indicators, K-12.*

Examination of a Curriculum Guide

Examining the curriculum guide of the school, district, or state for the grade level and/or subject area you are observing can help you better understand the materials that are being used in the classroom and the methods of instruction that are employed.

SAMPLE FORM 17

FORM FOR EXAMINING A CURRICULUM GUIDE

Examiner: Sam Ruloff

Date of Examination: November 22, 19—

Objective: To examine a curriculum guide and relate it to classroom curriculum

Instructions to the Examiner: Select a curriculum guide for the grade level and/or subject you will be observing. Complete this short answer survey.

1. Title of the guide: The Visual Arts Curriculum Guide
2. Check one: The guide is from the school____; the school district X ; the state____; other____ (specify)
3. Date of the guide: 1985
4. Grade level(s) of the guide: (7-9)–(10-12)
5. Subject area(s) of the guide: Art-Painting, Printing, Graphics, Ceramics, Jewelry, Sculpture, Commercial Design, Weaving

Answer the following yes/no or as indicated:

6. The guide includes: objectives Yes , student activities Yes , resources Yes , examples Yes , bibliographies Yes , computer software sources No , test banks No , discussion questions No , material for making transparencies No , content outlines No , other (specify) Procedures—Slides, Films, Visiting Artists

7. The guide suggests appropriate textbooks (specify): <u>Drawing with Ink, Creative Embroidery, The Picture History of Painting</u>
8. The guide suggests appropriate supplemental books. <u>Yes</u>
9. The guide suggests appropriate references. <u>Yes</u>
10. The guide suggests activities for different levels of students (i.e. gifted, advanced, basic, etc.) <u>Provides choices, in some areas. Suggestions for advanced/gifted.</u>

Examination of a Textbook

It is also useful to examine textbooks used for the grade level and subject area you are observing. Knowing what is in the textbooks helps you better understand the content of the lessons and the activities in which the students are involved. Below is a form to help you see how a student observer has examined a textbook.

SAMPLE FORM 18

SURVEY FOR EXAMINING A TEXTBOOK

Name of Examiner: <u>Myron Suksawat</u>

Date of Examination: <u>December 4, 19—</u>

School: <u>Brentwood Magnet</u>

Classroom Teacher: <u>Mrs. Inez Waxman</u>

Instructions to the Examiner: Complete the following either by writing <u>X</u> in the response where appropriate, by checking the blank space where appropriate, or by checking either yes or no.

1. Title of text: <u>HBJ Health</u>
2. Author(s): <u>Carolyn Burton, David Poehler, Romaine Sullivan, William Utter</u>
3. Publisher: <u>Harcourt, Brace, Jovanovich</u>
4. Year of publication: <u>1987</u>
5. Subject: <u>Health</u>
6. Grade level intended: <u>5th</u>
7. The text is part of a graded series. yes <u>X</u> no ____
8. Grade level(s) of the series (check one) K-6 ____; K-8 <u>X</u>; K-12 ____; 6-8 ____; 9-12 ____; other (specify) ____

9. The text has the following aids: a) objectives, yes ____ no X; b) marginal notes, yes X no ____; c) preview questions, yes ____ no X; d) tables and figures, yes X no ____; e) illustrations, yes X no ____; f) index, yes X no ____; g) review questions, yes X no ____; h) glossary, yes X no ____; other <u>Practice tests</u>

10. The teacher's manual for the text includes: a) lesson plans, yes X no ____; b) follow-up or supplementary activities, yes X no ____; c) transparencies, yes X no ____; d) duplicator masters, yes X no ____; e) tests, yes X no ____; f) resources, yes X no ____; g) other <u>objectives</u>

11. Tables, figures, and illustrations: a) are placed near the content they support, yes X no ____; b) supplement the narrative, yes X no ____; c) reinforce the narrative, yes X no ____; d) are attractive and motivating, yes X no ____

12. Student workbooks, if provided, a) correlate with the text, yes ____ no ____; b) supplement the text, yes ____ no ____; provide effective directions, yes ____ no ____ <u>No workbooks</u>

13. The content of the text is organized by a) units, yes X no ____; themes, yes ____ no X; b) topics, yes X no ____; c) chronological order, yes ____ no X; d) skills, yes ____ no X; e) objectives, yes ____ no X; f) other _____

14. The content of the text: a) is accurate, yes X no ____; b) relates to interests of students at this age level, yes X no ____; c) is readable by students of this age level, yes <u>not all</u> no ____; d) is motivating to students of this age level, yes X no ____

15. The following content in the text relates to a curriculum guide either of the district, state, or school. List appropriate content below:
<u>Food, Diet, Body Parts, Communicable Diseases</u>
<u>Feelings, Body, Drugs, Safety/Environment</u>

16. I would like to teach from this text: yes X no ____

17. Some comments and questions I would like to raise about this text are:
<u>Written to the students; Will it be updated to include AIDS education?</u>

A Survey of Media

Since so many teachers use films, videos, cassettes, filmstrips and other media in their classrooms, it is helpful for student observers to learn a methodology for examining them. The following checklist will help in the process. It is important to note not only the number of different types of media available, but also how a piece of equipment is used. Is it used with the entire group or with small groups? Do individuals have easy access to such things as computers and typewriters?

SAMPLE FORM 19

CHECKLIST OF TECHNOLOGY/MEDIA IN CLASSROOMS

Name of Observer: Mel Price

Date of Observation: December 11, 19—

School: Bethel Middle

Classroom Teacher: Mrs. King

Grade/Subject: Sixth grade

Objective: To observe the use of technology/media in the classroom and its use with individuals, small groups, and the whole group

Instructions to the Observer: After structured observation or an interview with the classroom teacher, put a check in the appropriate columns. Check if used with: I - Individual, SG - Small Group, WG - Whole Group.

Equipment	Number in Classroom	Stays in Classroom	Loaned from Media Center or Other Source	I/SG/WG
Projectors				
Overhead	1	✓		SG ✓ / WG ✓
Slide	1	✓		SG ✓ / WG ✓
Film	1		✓	WG ✓
Movie			✓	WG ✓
Opaque			✓	WG ✓
Tape Recorder(s)	2	✓		I ✓ / SG ✓ / WG ✓
Computer(s)	1	✓		I ✓
Record/ Cassette Player(s)	1	✓		I ✓ / SG ✓ / WG ✓
T.V.	1	✓		SG ✓ / WG ✓
Radio	1	✓		SG ✓ / WG ✓
VCR			✓	
Calculator(s)	20	✓		I ✓ / SG ✓ / WG ✓
Software	20+ programs	✓		I ✓ / SG ✓ / WG ✓
Typewriter(s)	2	✓		I ✓
Others (list)				

A Survey of Computer Software

Computer software is an increasingly common instructional tool in today's classrooms. Therefore, it is important that student teachers learn how to examine and evaluate it before using it in a classroom. Below is a simple guide for examining computer software.

SAMPLE FORM 20

SOFTWARE SELECTION GUIDE FOR COMPUTER-ASSISTED INSTRUCTION

Examiner: Ryan O'Donnell

Date of Examination: June 2, 19—

Software Title: The Medalist States

Publisher: Hartley

Date: 1982

Instructional Purpose: To learn important facts about states

Computer Compatibility: 48K Apple II, II+, IIc, IIe

Directions to Examiner: Rate the content, usability, and design aspects of the instructional package on a scale of 1 to 5 (1 is lowest and 5 is highest).

A. CONTENT

3   1.   Is the instructional content of the software appropriate to the established curriculum? (5th grade)

    3   a. Does the subject matter of the software address educational objectives that are appropriate for the students who will use it?

    5   b. Is the content accurate with no errors of fact or statement?

    5   c. Is the content presented in an unbiased manner?

    5   d. Is the program free of harmful generalizations and stereotypes based on sex, race, age, or culture?

3   2.   Is the program interesting and enjoyable to use?

    3   a. Is the instruction presented in a lively and interesting way?

    2   b. Are the graphics, color, or sound pleasing and conducive to instruction?

    4   c. Are program response times brief with a minimum of waiting time?

B. EDUCATIONAL DESIGN

5   1.   Is the program clear and logically organized?

3	2.	Can the user control the rate and type of instruction presented?
2	3.	Does the program present the new concepts or skills to be learned in a meaningful context?
3	4.	Does the program provide a sufficient amount of examples or illustrations to explain each new concept or skill?
1	5.	Does the program lead to higher level understanding or application?
5	6.	Does the program provide prompt instructional feedback?
5	7.	Does the program evaluate the user's progress?
2	8.	Do the evaluations allow diagnosis of the individual's weaknesses and strengths in the various instructional areas?
Y	9.	Can the evaluations be printed? (Y, N)

C. USABILITY

5	1.	Is the program easy to start and use?
5	2.	Is the program self-explanatory, not requiring dependence on a user's manual?
N	3.	Can the program disk be copied for multiple use? (Y, N)
5	4.	Is it easy to exit the program?

Designed by: James McGlinn, University of North Carolina at Asheville. Unpublished.

Student Assessments Used in the Classroom

Because students learn in a variety of different ways, it is important that teachers develop a variety of techniques for assessing student skills and progress. Below is a checklist to help student observers indicate the variety of tools used in the classroom to evaluate student work.

SAMPLE FORM 21

CHECKLIST TO DETERMINE STUDENT ASSESSMENTS EMPLOYED IN THE CLASSROOM

Observer: Loyda Chacon

Teacher: Mr. Ramos

Grade/Subject: 4th

School: Riverside Elementary

Date: December 2, 19—

Objective: To determine various assessment techniques

Instructions to Observer: After structured observation or interview with the classroom teacher, put a check in the appropriate column. *List additional assessments where required.

Type of Assessment	Observed	From Interview
1. Commercial Workbooks in Curricular Areas		
Reading	✓	
Mathematics	✓	
Science		
Social Studies		
Language Arts	✓	
Others* (handwriting)	✓	
2. Duplicated Sheets	✓	✓
3. Homework Assignments		✓
4. Oral Presentation/Report		✓
5. Hands-On Performance		✓
Computer	✓	
Science Experiment	✓	
Construction Project		✓
Dramatic Performances/Skits		✓
Chalkboard Work	✓	
Art Project	✓	
Musical Production	✓	
Classroom Displays/Bulletin Board	✓	
School Displays	✓	
Others*		
6. Written Work		
Reports	✓	
Research Projects		✓
Creative Writing	✓	
Others*		
7. Teacher-Made Tests	✓	
8. Prepared Tests From Students' Texts		✓
9. Standardized Tests		✓
10. State Competency Tests		✓
11. Anecdotal Records		✓
Writing Journals/Folders	✓	
Art Folders		✓
Cumulative Record Folders		✓
Others*		
12. Others*		

3

OBSERVING STUDENTS

ANECDOTAL OBSERVATIONS OF STUDENTS

Anecdotal observations of students can reveal many things. One student can be observed over a long period of time, in a variety of situations, or several different students can be observed on different occasions in the same classroom. Over a long period of time, changes can be seen in a student. It would be interesting to note, for example, differences in how Sammy, in the sample anecdotal record from below, responds in his mathematics class of average-ability students as compared to his history class of above-average students. It would also be beneficial to note how his behavior in the history class changes from day to day and month to month. It might also be instructive to observe several students of differing abilities in Sammy's history class. What is the ability level of Jennifer, the girl who helps Sammy? How does she respond in this class? What are her interactions like with other students in the class? What about the boy who rolls his eyes at Sammy; what is his ability and interaction with other students?

SAMPLE FORM 22

ANECDOTAL RECORD FOR OBSERVING STUDENTS

Name of Observer: <u>Sally Reider</u>

Date and Time of Observation: <u>10/18/19—, 2:05–3:00 P.M.</u>

Length of Observation: <u>55 minutes, one class period</u>

Person and/or Event Observed: <u>Sammy Hayes, student</u>

Grade Level and/or Subject: <u>Tenth; American History</u>

Objective of Observation: <u>To see how an average-ability tenth grader responds in history classroom</u>

According to his teacher, Sammy Hayes is an average-ability tenth grader. Although he is average in ability, based on standardized test scores, Sammy is one of those students who works diligently. I am observing Sammy's tenth-grade history classroom. His teacher suggested that today would be a good day to observe Sammy because the students are working in small groups and Sammy usually contributes well to the group. So that Sammy does not know I am particularly observing him, I will sit outside the group, but in a place where I can hear the students' interactions.

The bell rings. Sammy comes into the room quietly. The teacher pointed Sammy out to me yesterday so that I could quickly spot him. He's an average-looking kid: average height, slight build, teenage complexion (but not acne), medium-length brown hair— looks a bit greasy today. His clothes are typical, too: bleached blue jeans and a white tee shirt, running shoes without socks. Sammy does not stand out. He is neither attractive nor unattractive. Although he does not appear to be particularly outgoing, he is also not shy. He looks like the kind of kid who could easily get lost.

He sits down at his desk while many of the students mill around the room, but he is not a loner. He is talking to the boy sitting next to him, and the girl in front has turned around to ask him something. It appears she's asking him something about the assignment, since she's finding a page in his textbook.

The bell rings. Most of the students go to their seats. The teacher must remind a few of them that it's time to sit down. Sammy continues to talk quietly to the girl in front of him, but looks up and gets quiet when the teacher looks at the class and says, "All right, class, today we're going to work in our groups to prepare for our oral presentations. But, before we do so, hand your homework up to the person in the seat in front of you. Yes, Sammy?" Sammy says, "Katie and I were just talking about our homework, and we don't know what numbers we were supposed to do. I thought it was 1, 3, and 7 and Katie thought it was 1, 3, and 9." A boy in the front says, "That's because we had a choice for the last question!" "That's right," the teacher says to Sammy, "You and Katie are both right. Now will you hand in your homework?" Sammy hands his to Katie.

I should probably say here that Sammy's teacher told me that this is a college prep class, and Sammy is one of the less able students in the class, but he tries so hard that the guidance office decided to place him in it. However, the teacher says he thinks Sammy is beginning to get frustrated. For all his trying, he's only getting "C's." In his other, less competitive classes, he gets "A's."

The teacher tells the students to get in their groups as they did on Monday, and to have one group member go to the bookshelves and pick up the material they were working on. He reminds them that they should take all their material with them and only move the desks nearest where their group is supposed to meet. He also reminds them that this group project counts for ⅓ of their grade for this unit. These are good kids and they follow his instructions, although there seems to be some confusion at the bookshelves. The teacher goes over to straighten it out.

Sammy has moved to his group and is asking another student what they are supposed to be doing today. The student rolls his eyes and says, "We're supposed to finish what we started on Monday." Sammy still looks puzzled, but doesn't pursue it.

The room is noisy, and the teacher says, "O.K., folks, you should have your materials. Now, get back to your group and get started. If you have questions, have one group member raise a hand and I'll get to you as soon as I can." Three groups already have hands up. No one in Sammy's group has raised a hand.

The girl who was getting the group's materials returns to Sammy's group and begins to hand things out from the box she has picked up. She gives Sammy a book. Sammy frowns. "What am I supposed to do with this?" he says. "Wait, Sammy," the girl says, "we haven't started yet." Most of the group members begin looking things up. One boy is drawing a map of what appears to be a battlefield. Several others are talking and laughing. Sammy is just sitting, staring at the book. Leadership seems to be lacking in this group. Finally, one of the boys says to Sammy, "Hey, Sammy, you're supposed to be looking up information about the Battle of Gettysburg." Sammy's eyes light up in recognition, and he immediately gets busy. I can't help but notice that he does not appear to know how to look things up in an index; he's looking in the table of contents. After some time, he finds an appropriate chapter and turns to it. He begins thumbing through the chapter. When he finally finds something, he calls out, "Wow, did you know how many Union soldiers were killed at Gettysburg?" One student looks over Sammy's shoulder at the passage and says, "Wow!" Another student says, "Sammy, you're supposed to be writing those things down. Remember the mimeographed sheet from Monday? You need to fill it out so we can compile all the information for our chart. Remember?" "Oh, yeah," says Sammy. He begins looking for the sheet. The girl who'd looked over his shoulder, says, "I think it's in the box, Sammy; mine was." Sammy goes to the box to look and finds his sheet way on the bottom. His name is on it, but little else. Several of the students who are doing other battles are nearly through. Sammy begins diligently searching. Some of the other students begin to report their data to put on the chart. One boy says to Sammy, "Who was the commanding officer for the South at Gettysburg?" Sammy says, "I haven't found that yet." The boy rolls his eyes, but the girl next to Sammy says, "I've finished most of mine; your battle is harder. Let me help you look for it." Sammy smiles, and they begin to work together. The teacher walks by, sees the group is working, and starts to move on. He looks at Sammy's paper and sees that he's barely begun. "What's the problem, Sammy?" he asks. Sammy shrugs. "Can I help?" the teachers asks. "No, I can do it," Sammy says looking down. The girl says to the teacher, "Sammy's got the hardest battle; I'll help him because I finished." "Thank you, Jennifer," the teacher says. (I like this Jennifer girl; I'll need to ask the teacher about her.) Sammy and Jennifer continue to work together. Sammy is now smiling. The rest of the group is ignoring them as they continue to list on the chart facts from the other battles.

[The observation continues in this fashion.]

Shadowing a Student

A simple, but time-consuming anecdotal technique for determining what it is like to be a particular student in a particular school is shadowing that student throughout an entire school day. From this process, the observer can learn how the student interacts with teachers and other students, how the student handles social and academic situations, what the student does with his or her non-class time, what a day in the life of a student in the particular school is like, etc.

Before shadowing a student, it is essential to obtain permission from the student, since it is an intrusion in his or her life (not necessary with elementary school students), the teacher(s) of the student, the principal, and, in some cases, the student's parents or guardians. The observer should carefully explain that the goal of the shadowing is not to analyze the individual, but rather to determine what it is like to be a student at the individual's school. The observer should encourage the student to behave as naturally as possible, explaining that the shadowing will not be as helpful to the observer if the student acts differently than usual or tells his or her friends of the observation. The observer should ask the student to try to ignore him as much as possible and should simply follow the student's schedule, remaining as unobtrusive as possible.

In classrooms, the observer should sit out of the line of sight of the majority of the students. In the lunchroom, the observer should sit where the student can be observed, but where the observer cannot be seen by the student. If possible, the observer should talk with the student at the end of the day, sharing observations, not judgments, and asking about the student's perception of school, peers, subjects, likes and dislikes. A separate shadowing form should be completed for each lesson and/or separate time period (i.e., classes, lunch, recess) during the day.

SAMPLE FORM 23

SHADOWING FORM

Name of Shadowed Student: <u>Natasha Reynolds*</u>

Observer: <u>Sally Burke</u>

Date: <u>9/4/19—</u>

Time: <u>8:30-10:20</u>

Grade: <u>12th</u>

Subjects: <u>German/English</u>

Objective: <u>To understand what it is like to be a student at East Rodgers H.S.</u>

General Description of Location: <u>Classrooms—German II/German III—28 students (8 girls, 20 boys); English—30 students (16 girls, 14 boys)</u>

Instructions to the Observer: Select a student to shadow for an entire school day. Use a separate page for each class period or segment of the school day you observe. Every five to fifteen minutes, record what the subject of the observation is doing; also indicate what other students and teachers are doing. At the end of the day, summarize the shadowing. If possible, interview the student and report the results.

Subject/Class: German

Time (recorded every five to fifteen minutes)	What Subject Was Doing	What Classmates and Teacher Were Doing
8:30-8:35	talking to neighbor	T. tells class to be quiet for morning announcements. Most students talking.
8:35-8:45	translated sentence into literal English—sounded bizarre	T. trying to help students correct quiz from day before. T. told personal anecdotes. Most of class amused.
8:45-8:50	put head on desk	"
8:50-9:00	answered question	"
9:00-9:10	talked to neighbor, put head down	"

Subject/Class: English

Time	What Subject Was Doing	What Classmates and Teacher Were Doing
9:20-9:35	worked on quiz	T. gave quiz on assignment. All but one student worked diligently. He didn't write any answers.
9:35-9:40	Answered question # 4	T. let students correct own papers.
9:40-9:45	head down on desk	
9:45-9:50	Appeared to listen to others reading orally	Students took turns reading orally.
9:50-10:00	Read silently, put head down, then up, then read again	T. gave directions to read William Bradford's "Of Plymouth Plantation." Most students read quietly, some talked.
10:00-10:10	Answered two questions about what she had read	T. asked questions about content of silent reading. Most students knew the answers. T. paraphrased what students had read.
10:10	closes book; gets out of seat	T. assigns questions in text for homework

The following should be completed at the end of the shadowing:

Overview (summarize how the student seemed to be involved, how the student interacted with teachers and peers, what the student seemed to learn, how the student seems to feel about the class)

Overview — Natasha didn't appear to be that interested in the German class. I got the impression from Natasha that she took the class because she thought it would be easy for her since her mother is German. She was more attentive in the English class especially when she could answer questions. She did seem to lose some interest when reading silently.

Report of interview with student:

(Lunch time outside on picnic table)—Natasha asked me several questions about college. She said she'd like to go there someday. She said history and English were her favorite subjects, but not her favorite classes. Her major complaint about school was not enough time for lunch or in between classes to socialize. Natasha said she liked horses and some day hopes to "own and manage a rehabilitation horse barn."

*The name of the shadowed student and the school have been changed.

Anecdotal Profile of a Student

This technique is similar to, but less time-consuming than, shadowing. It allows the observer to study two or more students during a single lesson.

The goal of the anecdotal profile is to examine the attitudes and activities of several students during a specified period of time. The observer should select two or three students to observe for fifteen to twenty minutes each. It is helpful if these students appear to be quite different in terms of certain key characteristics (e.g., appearance, sociability, or academic achievement). Since the observation of the students is for a limited time period, the observer should record the students' activities and attitudes every one to two minutes, rather than every five minutes as in the shadowing study. These observations can be kept on 3" × 5" index cards. An example follows:

SAMPLE FORM 24

PROFILE CARD OF STUDENT 1

Observer's Name: Monica Williams

Student's Name: Jason Maxwell

Date: 12/5/19—

Time: 9:30-9:40

Subject/Grade: Reading Group of 5; 3rd

Location: Classroom

Number of Students Observed: 1

Time (recorded every minute)	Student's Activities/Attitudes
9:30-9:32	Adjusts chair; moves body left to right; whispers to friend next to him on his left.
9:32-9:34	Looks at reading chart; raises hand. Stands up, responds "Divide between the two consonants."
9:34-9:36	Raises hand again when not called on, says, "I knew that, too." Plays with book on lap.
9:36-9:38	Opens book; appears to be reading silently; sometimes moves lips.
9:38-9:40	Raises hand again and says, "I know, I know." When not called on, appears to sulk.

PROFILE CARD OF STUDENT 2

Observer's Name: Monica Williams

Student's Name: Maggie Reid

Date: 12/5/19—

Time: 9:45-10:00

Subject/Grade: Reading Group of 5; 3rd

Location: Classroom

Number of Students Observed: 1

Time (recorded every minute):	Student's Activities/Attitudes
9:45-9:47	Raises hand; says: "the boy wanted to help the old man." Smiles at person on her right. Plays with hair, makes noise with her shoes.
9:47-9:49	Appears to listen to others' responses. Plays with her hair. Asks, "Can I read that part out loud?"
9:49-9:51	Closes book; puts it under chair. Picks up workbook and pencil. Turns pages looking for right page. Scowls and says, "We did this before."
9:51-9:53	Takes pencil; puts an X after phrases in book. Works fast and says, "It's the same but different."

STRUCTURED OBSERVATION OF STUDENTS

There are many types of structured observations that can reveal specific information about students. Descriptive profile charts are more specific and focused than the anecdotal profiles discussed above. Coding systems allow observers to tally elements of student behavior. Informal inventories of students allow observers to gain data about students from the students' perspectives. Sociograms assist observers in plotting the interaction of students in a social environment such as a classroom.

Descriptive Profiles of a Student

Descriptive profiles are very similar to anecdotal profiles, but are more complete in that they attempt to record a continuing collection of facts to describe a particular phenomenon. The recordings are made without regard to their meaning, value, or use. A descriptive profile always begins with the date, time, and place, and includes statements and explanations of the background of the situation or setting. Descriptions tell what happened, who did or said what, and how it was done. They are noted as objectively and completely as possible. Direct quotes are recorded, posture and facial expressions are described, gestures and voice quality are noted. However, interpretations are avoided. For example, "his eyes flashed, he frowned, his body became rigid, and his fist was clenched," rather than "he was angry" (Perkins, 1969, p. 28). The descriptive profile is not unlike what a writer attempts to do when setting a scene in a literary work. The author attempts to show the readers the scene, to make the readers feel as if they are there. The author attempts to keep out of the scene, and, therefore, shows rather than tells. The descriptive profile should do the same thing.

In descriptive profiles, observations should be limited to only a few phenomena at a time. Descriptive observers can make their jobs easier if they look for specific elements of a personality or environment. For example, the descriptive profile chart below outlines one student's actions during a lesson. The observer is looking for how and when the student is actively involved in the lesson, and how and when she is not.

SAMPLE FORM 25

DESCRIPTIVE PROFILE CHART

Plotted by: Sarah Cardinalli

Date: 10/28/19—

Student Observed: Melissa Hernandez

School: <u>Smith Elementary</u>

Grade: <u>2nd</u>

Interval: <u>20 seconds</u>

Background: <u>Poor student; limited behavior problems</u>

Instructions to Observer: Record brief phrases to indicate the activities of the student during discussion and work periods. Place student activities under "application" if they show involvement in the lesson; place under "distraction" if they do not show involvement in the lesson.

Discussion Period		Work Period	
Application	**Distraction**	**Application**	**Distraction**
Listened to teacher.		Opened workbook. Looked at work.	
	Fiddled with pencil.	Raised hand.	Frowned.
Listened, shook head.			Doodled.
	Played with fingernails.		Talked to neighbor.
Looked at book.		Looked at workbook. Raised hand. Doodled.	Frowned.
Answered question.			
		Listened to teacher.	
Asked question. Read assignment on board.		Looked at book.	Played with fingernails.
	Looked at fingernails.	Picked up pencil.	
	Talked to student next to her.	Wrote in book.	Frowned. Put head on desk.
Looked at teacher; raised hand.			
	Looked at student.		
Asked question. Listened to answer.			

Adapted from John Devor, *The Experience of Student Teaching*, 1964.

Coding Systems of Student Participation

Another simple tool to help observers limit what they are looking for in a classroom is the coding system. A coding system looks for specific elements within the classroom. Usually, the observer codes the extent of the presence of these elements on 3″ × 5″ file cards. The most frequent use of this technique is in the observation of students and teachers. Just as in other observational tools, the observers must know what they are looking for before designing the coding system.

In the example of a coding system below, the observer is looking for the extent of participation of various students in the lesson. Cards could be made to record the participation of several students during a single lesson. Over a period of time all students' participation could be coded.

SAMPLE FORM 26

CODING SYSTEM TO OBSERVE STUDENT PARTICIPATION IN LESSONS

Observer: Sally Reider

Student: Sammy Hayes

Grade: Tenth

Date: 10/18/19—

Topic: Civil War

Interval: 20 seconds

Directions: Place a slash in appropriate column to indicate student activities during a single lesson.

Important Contributions	Minor Contributions	Distracting Remarks
I I	卌 I	I I I

Informal Inventories of Students

Another simple technique for gathering data about students is to develop inventories that would list the interests of students, their favorite teachers, how students view themselves, how they view the school, and the subjects they take. Almost anything you want to learn about the students can be asked on an informal inventory. Many inventories are available through educational publications. However, the inventories that are the most valuable to observers are those designed to meet the objectives of the specific class. Below is a simple interest inventory, designed by a student observer, to determine the student's interest in reading. Inventories can also be administered to a large group of students and tallied to learn the most common responses.

SAMPLE FORM 27

INCOMPLETE SENTENCE INVENTORY

Observer's Name: Irene Johnson

Student's Name: Billy Malone

Grade/Subject: Reading 4th

Date: 9/13/19—

Objective: To determine Billy's reading interests.

Instructions to the Observer: Determine the purpose of completing an informal inventory. Then design some incomplete sentences related to your objective. Also provide sample answer for number 1 in the instructions to the student.

Instructions to the Student: Complete each sentence below as honestly and completely as possible. For example, you might complete number 1 as follows: When I get home from school I usually play outside.

1. When I get home from school I usually get a snack.
2. On rainy Saturdays I particularly like to do puzzles.
3. When I am at home in the summer, I like to play ball.
4. When I go to the beach or pool, I always take with me: my ball, my friend, Jim.
5. When I was a small child I remember my mother read to me.
6. When I was a small child I remember my father _____. (Billy did not complete this sentence).
7. The best book I remember reading is about snakes.
8. I like to read the magazine National Geographic.
9. The last book I read was The Fascinating World of Bees.

Peer Group Interaction: Sociograms

For most students, interactions with peers is exceedingly important. In fact, by middle or junior high school, interaction with peers takes precedence over all other interactions. Therefore, it is helpful to discover ways to observe and analyze how students relate to each other. Perhaps the easiest technique for accomplishing this is the sociogram.

A sociogram graphically examines how the students in the class feel about each other. It indicates which students are most liked by other students and which are isolated from other students. Completion of a sociogram requires the cooperation of the classroom teacher.

To complete a simple sociogram, the observer or the classroom teacher should have students list three classmates with whom they would like to be associated socially. For example, students can be told, "On our field trip next week, we will be in groups of four. Please list the three other students, in order of preference, that you'd most like to be grouped with for the trip." It should be made clear to students that the teacher cannot guarantee that all their suggestions for grouping will be followed, but their preferences will be used as a guide in helping to form the groups. The students' choices can be tallied on a chart such as Sample Form 28. The names of students in the class are listed both vertically and horizontally. In the vertical list the students are considered choosers. The order in which they have selected companions is given in the horizontal box next to the person's name. At the bottom of the form is a place to tally the total number of choices per student.

SAMPLE FORM 28

TALLY CHART OF STUDENT GROUP SELECTIONS

Chosen / Choosers	Pam	John	David	Steve	George	Brian G.	Paul	Scott J.	Scott K.	Jeff	Ruth	Marc	Libby	Sherman	Sharon	Tony	Judy	Alan	Brian S.	Jane	Wayne	Bill	Keith	Sandy	Lane
Pam													1		2		3								
John*																									
David				3	2											1									
Steve					1																3			2	
George												1				2					3				
Brian G.		1														2						3			
Paul												1	2								3				
Scott J.					2					1											3				
Scott K.					2											3						1			
Jeff				3															2			1			
Ruth												1									3				2
Marc					1													2	3						
Libby	3		0		2																			1	
Sherman					2											1					3				
Sharon	3									1							2								
Tony		1																			3				
Judy	3											1													2
Alan					1														2	3					
Brian S.					2													1		3					
Jane				3							1	2													
Wayne					2							1						3							
Bill					2		3																1		
Keith		2	3																				1		
Sandy					2							1									3				
Lane											1						2						3		
Chosen 1		1	1			1	2			1	3	4	2		1	2		1			3	1	1	1	1
2		1				2	7					1	1		1	2	2	1	2				1		2
3	3			3	1					1						1	1	1	2		4	1		1	
Totals	3	2	1	3	1	3	9	0	1	1	3	5	3	0	2	5	3	3	4	0	9	4	2	2	2

* John absent

From: Frederick J. McDonald, *Educational Psychology*, 2nd Ed., Wadsworth Publishing, 1965, p. 634.

In order to graphically illustrate which students are more popular than others socially, a sociogram can be constructed based on the information obtained in the tally chart. In Sample Form 29, for example, boys are drawn in circles, girls in squares. Arrows are drawn to each student selected, with the number of his selection marked as first, second, or third. Dotted lines indicate those students who selected each other. The larger circles and squares represent those who were selected more often than others.

SAMPLE FORM 29

SOCIOGRAM BASED ON CHARTED STUDENT PREFERENCES

Directions to Observer: Using the tally chart of student group selections, put the names of those students selected most in a prominent place on the page. Identify males by placing name in a circle, females by placing names in boxes. Then put names of students selected by these few next to them. If they selected each other, connect them with a dotted line. If not, draw an arrow to the student selected. Proceed in this fashion until all names are represented on the form.

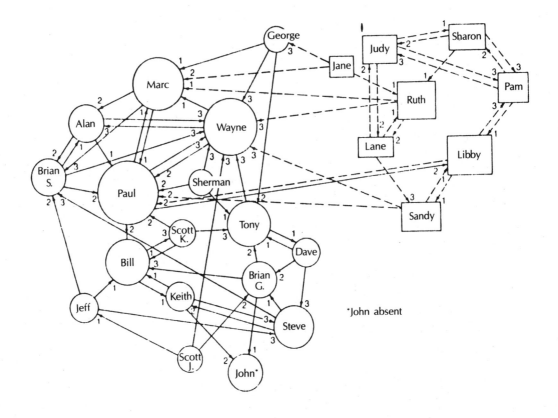

From: Frederick J. McDonald, *Educational Psychology*, 2nd Ed., Wadsworth 1965, p. 635.

PART II

Participation In the Schools

4

DEVELOPING SUCCESSFUL
TEACHING SKILLS

THE IMPORTANCE OF FIELDWORK

A survey of teachers, conducted by Louis Harris for the Metropolitan Life Insurance Company in 1985, found that

> former teachers . . . and current teachers . . . are in agreement about the steps they think will help most to produce good teachers in the future. More than 50% of both groups think these steps will help a lot: upgrading accreditation standards for teacher training programs at college; upgrading admission standards for students entering teacher training programs; and *requiring new teachers to serve a supervised apprenticeship or internship before being certified.* [Emphasis added] In addition, 50% of current teachers and 48% of former teachers think that placing more emphasis during teacher training on teaching skills, rather than subject skills, will help a lot.

Although this survey shows agreement among teachers about what is important in their training, the percentages also reveal areas of disagreement. However, there is little disagreement among practicing teachers, teacher educators, and critics of the profession that working in classrooms prior to teaching is essential.

Educational research supports this belief. A study of forty pre-student teachers, conducted by George Austin-Martin, Diana Bull, and Charlotte Molrine, found that pre-student teaching field experiences positively affected prospective teachers' interpersonal skills (1981). These interpersonal skills included working with students, other teachers, and administrators. In another study, educational researcher Dennis Sunal reported that preservice elementary teachers who participated in field experiences as well as methods studies were better able to model specific teacher roles than their peers who had not participated in the field experiences (1976). According to a research study conducted by Marvin Henry, Indiana State University students who were participating in a program that required field experiences as teaching aide-observers (20–30 hours), as teaching assistants (ten hours minimum), and as reading tutors (ten hours minimum), were better prepared than their peers who had not participated in the field experiences. The students who participated in the field experiences felt more confident of their ability to assist students with reading problems. They perceived themselves as better prepared to teach disabled students. In addition, they experienced fewer problems during student teaching (1988).

Although most people agree on the importance of school-based field experiences for preservice teachers, they frequently disagree on how much field experience is appropriate, when in the student's program it should occur, and what should be accomplished. The trend in contemporary teacher education programs is toward increasing the number of hours spent in the schools, beginning field experience early in a student's program, and requiring a greater variety of experiences than in the past.

Observation and Teaching Log

Observer: Michael Kealohalan Anderson
Grade: Fourth
January 3, 19____
First day of school

Oh, my goodness, so many unusual names to remember. The students seem to be excited to be back at the school. The schedule of the day is complicated (new to me). Students change classes at certain times during the day. Each teacher has a specialty that he or she teaches. Regardless of the specialty of the individual, each teacher must teach reading, spelling, and their specialty to their homeroom class. For example, my cooperating teacher [Ms. Owenbey] teaches reading, spelling, and computers to her homeroom. Then at 10:25 the students change classes. Then Ms. Owenbey teaches computers the remaining periods of the day.

January 4, 19____
Rain and rain. It's been raining for days now.
Today I took the "roll." It is really helping me learn the students' names. After spelling and reading, we had health. Oh, what a long day this has been. Health surely could be covered in the science class.

January 7, 19____
Nice weekend, no rain, however it is raining today. Yuk. The children seem to be getting back into the groove of school. Overall, I would say they seem to tolerate it without too much resistance.

January 8, 19____
Ms. Owenbey showed me how the students worked together on their "spelling kit." It is an interesting setup. The students are placed in pairs according to their ability to spell. They then go over lists of words out loud—taking turns of course. Then they each give one another a test by calling the words out while the other writes them down. This list is then checked by having the student call back the words they have spelled and checking for mistakes. The words misspelled are put on a separate piece of paper for further study. The students

switch roles and go through the process again. After approximately 20 minutes, the teacher calls time and all the students go over their review sheets. I like the procedure, and it does seem successful in producing capable spellers.

January 14, 19____
Today I brought two of my pet mice to school. They are a hit! Most of the students are rather apprehensive about them. One boy (Erick) is quite knowledgeable about rodents in general. I now know all the kids by first name. Most of them know my name too. . . .

January 17, 19____
I followed my class around all day today. We began our day with reading and a handwriting exercise. Then at 9:45 we went to art. From there we went to math. The students went over some sample math exercises involving multiplication and division of small or single-digit numbers and some double-digit numbers. From then we went to social studies where the students were reviewing for a test the following day. After lunch the class went to science; here they were being read to by the teacher about electrons and protons. After science the class moved to English. Here the English teacher had the students write in their journals about "winter time." Of all the lessons I observed this day I enjoyed the English lesson best of all. At 1:45 the students went to computer lab, where they had free choice of the program they would like to work with. Overall, I would say the day was sort of boring. With the exceptions of reading, art, computer, and English. It's no wonder the students go crazy when they get a free moment. They work in each class and have homework in all of them if they fail to complete their in-class assignments. . . .

January 23–24, 19____
The days are running together now. My responsibilities are that of an observer and occasional participant. Most of my participation occurs in reading and computer lab. In reading the students are all reading for a "Bookit Goal." This is a program done by Pizza Hut. Each month the students must read five books. The teacher verifies this by having the students retell the stories: main character, plot, etc. I listen to the students who have read short stories in their basal reader. They tell me the story. I grill them very thoroughly, demanding to know higher level associations such as: why do you think the character chose to respond the way he did? In computer the students do drills and exercises. They are then rewarded with some sort of game. They seem really content with this. Yet, I am not so sure I really go along with all of it. I think there should be programs that "grade" the students' progress, for example, with multiplication and division. The days are flying past now. I have been riding my bike to school every day it's not raining. The children are going crazy, wanting to know where I park it. I tell them I have been parking it in the "Bat Cave." I love it, and it's driving them crazy. The kids are great! I am still having a blast. . . .

February 11, 19____
The mother mouse had babies. Tiquanna and I predicted the correct number. The children are jazzed up about the mice. I told the students I would be hanging with them for the next 12 weeks. . . .

February 21, 19____
So much happens each day. Sometimes I am overwhelmed. It is no wonder teachers burn out. We hit the deck running about 8:00 and don't stop until 2:30. Then we plan and prepare for the next day until 3:30 or so. Tomorrow is a big day. Dr. Arnold is coming by to watch me teach my lesson. I am prepared, yet a little apprehensive. Cindy [Ms. Owenbey] has been letting me do lessons off and on, so the children are aware of my role as their teacher. . . .

February 25, 19____
It worked great. I split the children into two groups and had them chorus-read. They struggled with it, but I feel with a little time we will be moving along a lot more smoothly. I emphasized that we are to improve our reading skills by keeping up with the group. They did struggle with the activity, but I think they did so because it was novel. Great Day!
[The log continues in this manner with Michael Kealohalan Anderson (called Lani) telling of his observations, his work with small groups and individuals, and his initial teaching experiences.]

Expanding Beyond Observation

School-based observation and teaching experiences are the bridge between the worlds of theory and practice. Throughout your education and psychology programs you will be examining theory: theories about how eight-year-olds learn, about the success of disabled youngsters in the regular classroom, about the best ways to group, about the most effective way to organize a lesson, about how to deal with disruptive students. . . . However, until you have had the opportunity to sit in a classroom and observe what occurs from the teacher's point of view, none of these theories will be real.

Therefore, observation—gaining knowledge and understanding—should come first. Once you have had the opportunity to reflect on the teachers, students, classrooms, and schools you have observed, as discussed in chapters one through three, you should begin using what you have learned in your own planning and teaching. For many of you, this will begin as early as your first class in education. For others it will not occur until much later in your teacher education program.

Observing a teacher can show you a great deal about how to teach, but it will not tell you how *you* will teach. Educator Philip Jackson relates a time when he was a principal and visited several nursery school classrooms. He noted how teachers bent down to the eye level of children, how they held books on their laps, reading upside down so the children could see. He thought he could probably teach nursery school. But as he talked to the teachers, he realized it was more than holding the book, bandaging the knee, and eyeballing the child. It was "seeing/reacting in a certain spirit or manner to a special portion of the world—rooms full of three- and four-year-olds" (1986, p. 88). According to Jackson, specific skills such as how to make playdough are important, but feeling and acting at home in a particular instructional milieu is essential for a true teacher. Until you have this experience, you will not know whether you feel at home with particular students in a particular educational setting.

A good analogy for the importance of early school-based teaching experiences is learning to fly an airplane. Initially, students pilots might use flight simulators to experience flying a plane, but very early in their training, they take command of the plane as the instructor watches and critiques. This does not mean the simulator stops serving a function for them. In fact, they will use it many times to simulate uncommon occurrences. However, nothing substitutes for the experience of actually flying the plane. Simulated teaching experiences—role-playing classroom experience with peers—will continue to be a helpful tool throughout your teacher training. But nothing will substitute for the experiences you gain in the classroom with real children and an effective practicing teacher serving as your evaluator and mentor.

Experience Alone Is Not Always a Good Teacher

For the preservice teacher, teaching and learning should go hand in hand. For example, those who first experience teaching in student-centered classrooms might think the students are off task and out of control if they are not familiar with the student-centered approach. They may come away from this experience saying, "This kind of classroom is not for me." However, if they had first studied the student-centered classroom, observed in one, and examined teaching techniques common in such environments, the experience might have been different. Their conclusions would be based on knowledge rather than on misinterpretations of what they had experienced.

Frequently novice teachers make incorrect assumptions about the success of lessons they have taught. For example, Hank believed a lesson was successful because the students were well-behaved and responsive to his jokes and questions. His conclusion may be misleading. Assume that Hank has spent little or no time preparing the lesson. However, because he is glib and funny, the students are well-behaved and appear to respond. Their behavior may have little or nothing to do with the lesson or with Hank. Perhaps the students are exceptionally well-behaved. Perhaps the classroom teacher has prepared them for Hank's teaching by telling them they must be on their best behavior, or by rewarding them for good behavior. Hank, like the cat who jumps on the cold stove, and assumes it always will be cold, assumes that students will always behave and respond positively to his teaching, and that he need not change anything in his preparation or approach.

This example is also miseducative in that Hank assumes that the only role of the teacher is to deliver lessons. He neglects to see the teacher setting realistic objectives and evaluating students on these objectives. If he continually fails to plan, how will he know what the objectives of his teaching are? If he has no objectives, how will he know if the students have learned what he's taught?

The Importance of Feedback in Early Teaching Experiences

Nothing is more important than good feedback about initial teaching experiences. Good does not necessarily mean positive. Good feedback for Hank might include a preteaching conference with the classroom teacher, Mr. Thornberg, to discuss the lesson. This conference could lead Hank to develop plans. Mr. Thornberg might ask: What will you be teaching today? What are your objectives for the lesson? How will you ensure the students are progressing toward the objectives? How will you determine if they have learned what has been taught?

If the preteaching conference does not lead to plan development, the after-teaching conference between Hank and Mr. Thornberg might. Mr. Thornberg tells Hank that he has a good rapport with the students. Then he asks these questions: What did you expect the students to learn from your lesson? What methods did you employ to ensure they learned it? How did you involve the students in their own learning? How will you evaluate what they have learned? How will you grade them on what occurred today? If Karen's mother were to come in and ask what Karen missed while she was absent, what would you tell her? Hank may now understand that he must do more than perform.

Unfortunately, the feedback preservice teachers receive can also be mis-educative. Most of us want to give positive feedback to our students, and, unlike the situation in an airplane cockpit, positive feedback about teaching is rarely dangerous. In fact, most teachers have discovered that positive feedback increases motivation and improves results. However, if preservice teachers accept positive feedback as the final truth, they may miss opportunities to gain valuable insight. To avoid this problem, you should always ask teachers who evaluate your classroom performance, "What would you have done differently?"

Overly negative feedback can be just as misleading. Sometimes classroom teachers expect preservice teachers to perform beyond their capabilities. This usually occurs because the classroom teacher is unfamiliar with the preservice teacher's education program. The classroom teacher may not understand that it is the preservice teacher's first class in education, or she may not know that the student is expected to be working only with individual children. To avoid this problem, the preservice teacher should acquaint the classroom teacher with the role he or she is expected to play. Other suggestions later in this book will help students avoid misunderstandings about roles.

PARTICIPATING IN CLASSROOMS

Working in the classroom should proceed in a series of gradual steps from observation to teaching, as it did for Lani Anderson in the observation and teaching log. After teacher education students have had the opportunity to observe and complete some initial interpretation of their observations, they can ease into their roles as teachers by assisting the classroom teacher in a variety of noninstructional routines. When teacher education students have mastered some of these routines, they can begin working with the teacher in the ongoing instructional activity of the classroom. Still later, teacher education students may begin to assume some limited teaching assignments that are carefully planned with the classroom teacher, such as individual tutoring and small group instructional work. Not until the students feel comfortable with these activities should they move on to assume primary responsibility for a fully planned lesson. Before teaching the lesson, careful planning with the classroom teacher is essential. These gradual steps will be discussed in chapters five and six.

5

PRETEACHING AND PLANNING

PRETEACHING ACTIVITIES

After observing and before teaching, there are numerous activities that can help student participants better understand the children, the classroom organization, and the teaching process. Lani, in the anecdotal observation in chapter four, discusses some of these: taking roll, bringing his pet mice to class, discussing teaching techniques with the classroom teacher, etc. Janet Joyce, in the anecdotal record of preteaching activities in this chapter, discusses others: helping the children with art projects, going to staff development meetings, taking field trips, putting up a bulletin board, working with the teacher's aide to develop a classroom management system, discussing students with the teacher and teaching specialists, and filling out a worksheet related to a field trip they had taken. In the first section of this chapter we will provide you with additional ideas for preteaching activities.

SAMPLE FORM 30

ANECDOTAL RECORD OF PRETEACHING ACTIVITIES

Name of Student Participant: Janet Joyce

Name of Teacher: Ms. Bennes

Grade Level and/or Subject: Second grade

Date: 2/22/19— to 3/15/19—

Objective: To record activities I participated in prior to teaching

Directions to Student Participant: Keep an account of the activities you participated in prior to actual teaching. Indicate how you felt about each day's events.

February 11, 19____
The thing I liked most about today was helping the kids with their valentine folders. I had never woven paper before. It was fun watching them do it. It was a great first day!

February 12, 19____
School was dismissed early for staff development. The kids were pretty excited about it. Ms. Bennes and I spent the afternoon talking with Ms. Loritch, the speech teacher, about several of our students.

February 13, 19____
Today was a full day! We went on a field trip to the Health Adventure. The kids learned a lesson on dental hygiene. It was great and the kids liked it too. This afternoon we had a surprise birthday party for Ms. Canty, the teacher's aide. The kids never gave the secret away (which was a miracle). Ms. Canty was surprised and the party went well.

February 14, 19____
The whole day was great! I helped the kids make their valentines and showed them the proper way of addressing them. They counted valentine candy. This afternoon they had their valentine party. It was fun, but I'll be glad when things get back to normal. . . .

February 19, 19____
I found a worksheet called "Dental Insurance." I think it would be a neat activity to do as a follow-up to the Health Adventure field trip. There is math included on the worksheet. The students have to figure the math problem in order to know what color to color a part of the picture. They will then write a letter to Dr. Trueluck, thanking him for paying their way to the Health Adventure. The letter is on the back of the picture. . . .

February 20, 19____
We went on another field trip this morning. We went to see the Elephant Walk downtown [the circus had come to town]. We walked to get there. I never knew how tiring it could be to walk five blocks with 16 kids. By the end of the day, I was so tired, I didn't think I would make it home. But I did, and I was sure glad to be home.

February 21, 19____
I taught my first spelling lesson today. It went O.K. I think it could have been better. I never taught a spelling lesson before, and I basically did it the way Ms. Bennes does. It just wasn't me. Maybe tomorrow will be a little better.

February 22, 19____
Today's lesson went a little better. I can still see where there can be a lot of improvement. I'm going to have to sit down and really think of a different twist to teaching spelling.

February 25, 19____
Today was pretty bad. The kids didn't want to listen, and they didn't. This afternoon I read a story to them, and they were all over the place. Ms. Bennes even said she had not seen them act this way before. Ms. Bennes and I talked to the ones who were misbehaving. I just can't imagine another day like this one.

February 26, 19____

Today was so much better! They listened, they were polite, they were almost little sweethearts. We did something different in spelling whch they seemed to enjoy, and I think that helped a lot. This was a great turnaround from yesterday. . . .

March 6, 19____

Today we had a statewide tornado drill. It was supposed to be at 9:30 but it wasn't until about 10:15. It made the morning very disorganized and we really didn't get a whole lot accomplished. This afternoon I will help some of the children with their science projects for the science fair on Friday. It should be fun and interesting. . . .

March 15, 19____

I got a lot done today. I put up a bulletin board, watered the kids' lima beans, made a spelling Bingo game, and cut out positive reward incentives.

[Janet Joyce's log continues in this fashion, discussing how she helps the children make rabbit masks and helps to give an I.Q. test. She also discusses her concern about a child who threatens to run away and commit suicide, and her worries about how to discipline the children when they misbehave. She and the teacher's aide develop a management plan. She discusses getting ready to teach a social studies unit in which the children develop their own questions based on the table of contents of a chapter in their textbook.]

Assisting the Teacher

An important early school-based step toward the teaching process is assisting the teacher in a variety of noninstructional classroom duties. It allows education student participants to apply some of what they have learned through their college classes and in-school observation without taking the primary responsibility for students before they are ready.

First the student participant and classroom teacher should discuss what type of assistance would be most helpful to the teacher and valuable to the class. There are hundreds of noninstructional duties in which teachers are involved every day. They include activities as diverse as taking attendance and placing student work on the bulletin board. Although most of these duties are routine, they support the important work of teaching and learning. Classroom routines usually can be placed in one of these categories: physical condition of the room, movement of the children, handling materials and papers, keeping records and reports, classroom procedures, special drills/classes/days (Crow and Crow, p. 285).

Many student participants incorrectly assume that these tasks are demeaning and prevent active participation in the classroom. On the contrary, these routines are essential to the management of the classroom, and the teacher who does not master them is rarely able to teach.

Initially, routine tasks assumed by the student participants should not directly involve the children. We have provided you with a checklist of some of these activities.

SAMPLE FORM 31

CHECKLIST OF ROUTINES FOR HELPING THE TEACHER

Name of Student Participant: Reggie Gomez

Name of Teacher: Mr. Downs

Grade Level and/or Subject: 6th/Science

Date: 9/11/19— to 10/24/19—

Objective: To participate in noninstructional classroom duties.

Instructions to Student Participant: All the duties listed below are important to the management of the instructional environment. You will need to learn to complete these simultaneously with teaching the students and managing the class. To help you learn to do so efficiently, complete all tasks appropriate to your teaching situation and indicate the date each is accomplished. Please have the classroom teacher sign this form when all appropriate activities have been successfully completed.

Activity	Date Completed
1. Make a seating chart.	9-11
2. Take attendance.	9-16
3. Run errands for the classroom teacher.	9-3
4. Help with classroom housekeeping.	9-3
5. Organize materials needed for a lesson.	9-26
6. Make copies of materials needed for the lesson.	9-18
7. Help pass out materials to the students.	9-4
8. Arrange a bulletin board.	10-3
9. Check out books from the library to be used by students in the classroom.	9-13
10. Check out media to be used in a lesson.	10-14
11. Make a chart or graph.	10-29
12. Make a transparency or stencil.	9-16
13. Run a film, filmstrip, videotape, etc.	10-21
14. Get supplementary materials needed for a lesson (e.g., magazine illustrations, pamphlets, maps, etc.)	9-16
15. Develop a bibliography for an upcoming unit.	11-4
16. Correct papers.	9-19
17. Set up or help set up a lab.	10-21
18. Write news/assignments on the chalkboard.	10-5
19. Set up a learning center.	11-18
20. Set up an experiment or a demonstration.	10-24
21. Obtain a speaker to come to class or help organize a class field trip.	11-15
22. Help gather materials for a class party.	11-22
23. Help make costumes for a class play.	10-24

24. Send out a class newsletter to parents.   did not do
25. Other (please list below):   10-26
Supervised playground, took children to bus

I certify that the student participant listed above has successfully completed all of the above activities that are appropriate to my classroom.

Mr. Downs
_____
(Classroom teacher's signature)

       After student participants have worked in classrooms for a few days and begun to learn the routine and know the children, they can broaden their activities to include those that directly involve the children. We have provided you with a checklist of some of these activities.

SAMPLE FORM 32

CHECKLIST OF ROUTINES INVOLVING STUDENTS

Name of Student Participant: Alex Gerstenberger

Name of Teacher: Mrs. Caudle

Grade Level and/or Subject: 8th/Social Studies

Date: 9/19/19— to 11/14/19—

Objective: To determine students' skills, motivation, interests in teaching/learning situation.

Instructions to Student Participant: All the activities listed below are important to the instruction of the students. You will need to learn to complete these simultaneously with teaching the students and managing the class. To help you learn to do so efficiently, complete all tasks appropriate to your teaching situation and indicate the date each is accomplished. Please have the classroom teacher sign this form when all appropriate activities have been successfully completed.

Activity	Date Completed
1. Orient a new student.	9-19
2. Help individual students with seat work.	9-11
3. Work with a club or student activity.	10-14
4. Assist a small group.	9-24

5. Work with an individual student in a lab (e.g., computer, language, science).   9-27
6. Assist a handicapped student.   10-18
7. Assist students with library research.   10-31
8. Monitor a test.   11-14
9. Collect money.   9-6
10. Hand out and collect materials.   9-6
11. Listen to an individual student read or recite a lesson.   9-26
12. Give a test or a quiz.   11-11
13. Assist young children with clothing.   N/A
14. Bring books or materials to share with the students.   10-15
15. Supervise students outside the classroom.   10-21
16. Read aloud or tell a story.   9-30
17. Help students in a learning center.   11-6
18. Accompany students to a school office, the bus, or the playground.   9-26
19. Attend a parent-teacher conference.   10-29
20. Work with the teacher in developing an IEP (Individual Education Plan) for a mainstreamed student.   11-8
21. Accompany students to before- or after-school programs.   Daily beginning 9-9
22. Help monitor the hallway, lunchroom, or playground.   "   "
23. Other (please list below):
Worked with small groups in computer lab for 30 minutes, two days a week.

I certify that the student participant listed above has successfully completed all of the above activities that are appropriate to my classroom.

Mrs. Caudle
_____
(Classroom teacher's signature)

PREPARING TO TEACH

Most uninitiated observers of the teaching process believe that teaching is lecturing to a large group of students. Many contend that anyone who has knowledge and can speak, can teach. These contentions are based on the assumption that to teach, the teacher must be perpetually on stage. Of course, this is only a small part of what a teacher does. In fact, many teachers rarely stand in front of a large group of children. And they may be excellent teachers.

Teaching involves the employment of many activities at once. In addition to the routine tasks described above, classroom teachers frequently find themselves teaching small groups of students while they are instructing individuals within the group.

At the same time, they may be observing the activities of other students in the classroom. If a teacher, for example, knows that four students are at the math center, and that one of them is likely to have difficulty with the new word problem added today, he makes a mental note to see if the student needs help as soon as he finishes with another group. The teacher is also aware of the students working on a science experiment at the back sink, and is listening carefully for any sound that might indicate that playing with water is more interesting than using it in the experiment. The teacher can hear the beeps and burps from the computers, so he knows that the students are busily engaged. He is also aware that in 15 minutes he must interrupt all this activity so that there is time to introduce the children to the new social studies unit before lunch. When he hears a knock on the door he is not surprised, and knows that the door monitor will open it. Jacob Kounin describes the teacher's simultaneous involvement in dozens of activities as "withitness" (1970). Being able to focus on so many activities at once is not easy, nor does it come naturally to the beginner. "Withitness" is a skill learned from considerable experience with the variety of activities that occur in the classroom.

To help develop this essential skill, student participants should begin their teaching experiences with the smallest unit of classroom instruction—tutoring a single student on a single skill or concept. From this they can proceed to working with a small group of students, initially using the classroom teacher's plan, as Janet Joyce does, and later using their own plans. When this has been successfully accomplished, they can tackle the teaching of a lesson to the entire class. This teaching might initially be done using the teacher's plan; afterwards, with the help of the teacher, developing their own plans. After significant practice using all of these teaching skills, the student participant should begin developing "withitness."

Planning to Teach

Before any teaching is done, whether it be tutoring a single child or teaching a lesson to the entire class, planning is essential. Planning for anything—a social function, what college to attend, where to go on vacation—can be a difficult task. All planning requires reviewing the past and anticipating the future. The consequences of failing to plan are usually more painful than the labor of planning. The consequences of an unplanned or poorly planned lesson include for the teacher: embarrassment, preoccupation with discipline, loss of control, and a poor evaluation by a superior; for the student: loss of interest, disruptive behavior, and limited or no learning. The anecdote that follows gives one teacher's account of a lesson with little or no planning.

"RUNNING ACCOUNT" OF AN UNPLANNED LESSON

Aim: To discuss digestion.
Procedure: A pupil will give a report which will lead to a class discussion.
Material: Mimeographed drawing of the digestive process in hands of the pupils, and a sketch on the board of the same process.

Teacher	Pupils	Supervisory comment
	Mr. Gale, the diagram on the board says it takes four days for digestion to take place. Isn't that wrong?	
The boy who copied it down for me made a mistake.	But, Mr. Gale, the mimeographed sheet you gave us reads the same way.	Teacher loses respect by failing to admit his error.
Well, then, it's wrong. It should be four hours. Let's forget that until I take the roll. (Calls off names one by one.)		Uneconomic use of time. Should have a seating chart.
John, get up here and give your report.	(Report, obviously copied from an encyclopedia, read in three minutes.)	Pupils are evidently not taught how to make or give a report.
Is that all? Read it again.	Do we have to take notes on this? Will we be tested on this?	Indicates lack of any organized procedure.
Certainly, everything we do here is important. Joan, you come to the board and take down important data in John's report.		Yet notebooks of pupils around me contain no science notes.
John, read your report.	I've read it twice. (Girl at board not clear as to what she is to do.)	Introduces a new procedure with no preparation of the class.
We'll finish this tomorrow. Get out some paper. I'm going to give you a quiz. Copy down these questions.	(Class is very noisy.)	Teacher improvising. Had no alternative plan worked out.
All right, not too much talking.		
There is too much noise here. There is no need for it.		
Now look! What is all this chattering about? Stop it.	You didn't teach us any of this.	Quiz evidently not prepared beforehand.

This is supposed to be a quiz. Would you mind moving apart a little?	(Pupils unconcerned and talk throughout the quiz.)	Teacher's lack of planning and procedure leading to chaos.
Do you know what you can put down on this paper—zero.		
Look! I'm getting fed up. Come to detention this afternoon.		Threats ineffective. Class does not respect or fear teacher.
Do you realize that you people cannot keep quiet for five minutes?		
All right, I'll collect the papers, and we will go into tomorrow's lesson.		Collects papers one by one.
Anybody know what a spectrum is?	Something like a color wheel. (Aimless discussion for about ten minutes.)	Teacher improvising.
Read this chapter tomorrow.		Assignment nebulous.
Quiet now! I am going to open the door to see if classes have been dismissed.		School has a bell system. Teacher cannot wait to escape from the noise.

From: Thomas J. Brown, *Student Teaching in a Secondary School,* 1968

In teaching, successful planning requires thorough knowledge of the content, an understanding of a variety of methods for presenting the content, and a knowledge of the psychological readiness of the pupils. Any teacher who assumes that learning ends with the baccalaureate degree is not likely to be very successful. Some subjects that teachers in the 1990s are expected to teach were not included in their own curriculum when they were students. For example, many teachers never had a course in computers, but they now must teach word processing, graphics, and computer programming. Therefore, one of the most important parts of planning is continuous study.

Developing Plans

Although planning is always time-consuming, it is not a difficult process. Planning is a skill involving a series of steps that can be taught and learned. Assuming the teacher has knowledge of the content to be taught and the students, the steps in planning are as follows:

Preplanning
(1) Examine school district, county, or state curricular guides.
(2) Determine which goal(s) (a goal is the learning end) you will address in the lesson.
(3) Select the topic of the lesson.
(4) Gather materials and examples.
(5) Identify what students already know or believe about the topic.
(6) Determine the duration of your lesson.

Planning
(1) Write the goal(s) you plan to address at the top of your plan.
(2) Develop specific short-term objectives for your lesson. (Objectives are what you hope the pupils will accomplish by the end of the lesson.)
(3) Select the materials you will use.
(4) Identify an appropriate teaching methodology.
(5) Arrange the materials in a logical sequence.
(6) Choose appropriate learning activities and experiences.
(7) Decide how learning will be assessed.

Preteaching
(1) Prepare class handouts, audiovisuals, etc.
(2) Prepare the classroom for teaching.
(3) Review your plan.

Using the steps outlined above, the following plan was developed by a student participant to meet a tenth-grade state literal comprehension goal: "the learner will identify *sequence* of events." This student used the Madeline Hunter lesson plan format (chapter 1, p. 19–20) in the design of her lesson. This and other lesson plan formats that can be used for designing lessons can be found at the end of this book, 33B and 33C.

SAMPLE FORM 33

MODEL LESSON PLAN

Name of Student Participant: Juan Gomez

Name of Teacher: Mrs. Ricardo

Grade Level/Subject Area: 10th/English

Date: 12-4-19—

Goal: The learner will identify sequence of events.

Objectives:
1. The learners will identify the sequence of events in a videotape of a popular television show, "Murder She Wrote."
2. The learners will identify the sequence of events, using the format established by the class, in the short story "Four and Twenty Blackbirds" by Agatha Christie.

Materials:
1. Videotape player and television.
2. The videotape of an episode of "Murder, She Wrote."
3. Chalk.
4. 25 copies of *Adventures in Appreciation*, literature text containing Christie story.
5. Five sheets of newsprint, five magic markers, masking tape.
6. Overhead projector, blank transparency, and marker pen.

Duration: Two sixty-minute class periods.

Instructions to the Student Participant: Whether your plan covers several classroom sessions or only one, each lesson should include the steps listed below.

First Class

1. Anticipatory Set

Today we're going to be seeing a videotape of a recent episode of "Murder, She Wrote." (This alone will provide the motivation.)

How many of you have seen that show on T.V.?

Who is the main character of the show? (Jessica Fletcher, a mystery writer/detective.)

What usually hapens in the show? (List responses on chalk board—Be sure students determine the following: murder usually occurs early in the show. During the rest of the show, we are introduced to various suspects, learn their motives and alibis. Jessica spends her time searching for clues such as the murder weapon. Throughout the show we are presented with many "red herrings," leading us to the wrong conclusion. By the end of the episode the murder is solved. Write **SAVE** on the board; this will be needed tomorrow.) [5 minutes]

2. Objective

We will be looking for the exact sequence of events in today's episode. You'll need a notebook and a pen. Put everything else under your chairs. Write down each event as it occurs; you might want to use the outline on the board to assist you in the process. Remember, you are looking for the exact sequence of events. Be sure to take careful notes because you will need them in class tomorrow. (Wait for students to have notebook and pen on desk and everything else under their chairs.) [5 minutes]

3. Teacher Input

View the video of "Murder, She Wrote." (Watch video from rear of the room to monitor students' attention and note-taking.) [45 minutes]

Second Class
4. Checking for Understanding

Take out the notes you took yesterday on the "Murder, She Wrote" video. Put everything else under your chairs.

Let's review the sequence we recorded on the board yesterday. (Call students' attention to sequence written on board.)

Did you see a similar sequence in this episode? [5 minutes]

Did you find any "red herrings"? [5 minutes]

5. Guided Practice

You will be outlining the specific events of this episode in your activity groups. (Students are assigned to long-term activity groups, and they know the procedure to be used in completing group work.) The assignment for your group work is written on the board.

Assignment on the Board as Follows:
Group Work Assignment
1. Select a recorder.
2. List on the newsprint provided the sequence of events in the episode of "Murder, She Wrote." Be sure to include all elements outlined on the board.
3. You have ten minutes to complete this task. When you have finished, post your newsprint on the side wall, using the masking tape provided.

(While students are working in groups, place a copy of the literature anthology under each chair.)

After groups have completed their sequence of events charts, compare each sequence chart with the class. On the overhead projector, create a class sequence of events. Discuss why some groups sequenced the events of the story differently. [25 minutes]

6. Independent Practice

Now we will independently read Agatha Christie's "Four and Twenty Blackbirds," found in your literature anthology on page 16.

Have any of you heard of Agatha Christie before? Have you read anything by her? (She is a famous British mystery writer, known particularly for her murder mysteries. The detective in this story is one of her two famous detectives, Hercule Poirot. He is a Frenchman who is always investigating cases in London.)

As you read this story, outline the sequence of events just as we did for "Murder, She Wrote." I'll leave the original outline of the sequence of events we did yesterday on the board to help you. I'll also leave the one we just completed on the overhead to help you. You'll need to do this in your notebook. We'll have about 20 minutes to read today in class. If you do not finish the story, you'll need to finish it for homework. I will be collecting the sequence you do for this story tomorrow at the beginning of class. (This will be used to assess the students' understanding of the concept of sequence of events as well as their understanding of Christie's story.) Any questions? (As students are reading, put homework assignment on the board.)

Assignment on the Board as Follows:
Homework Assignment
1. Finish reading "Four and Twenty Blackbirds" by Agatha Christie (Adventures in Appreciation, pp. 16–25).
2. On notebook paper list the **sequence** of events of the story.
3. Assignment will be collected at beginning of class period tomorrow. [25 minutes]

7. Closure

Five minutes before the end of the class, ask the students to stop reading and pay attention to a brief discussion.

Summarizing questions:
How was this story similar to the episode of "Murder, She Wrote"?
Did the sequence follow the model we put on the board?
How did the story differ from the episode of "Murder, She Wrote"?
Did Christie present you with any "red herrings"?

Your assignment for tomorrow is on the board.

*lesson plan format based on the work of Madeline Hunter.

The student participant who taught the lesson in a tenth-grade English class understood, with the help of the classroom teacher, that it would lead to several more complex lessons. A unit (a series of lessons addressing a single topic) on mystery writing was planned for several weeks later, and the lesson described in this chapter was used as an advance organizer for the unit to help students understand the plotting techniques used by mystery writers. During the unit, the tenth-graders would also write their own narratives, learning to employ sequencing techniques. Likewise, they would examine plot sequence in a variety of other literary genres, including fantasy, historical fiction, and adventure/suspense.

The sequencing of lessons in an entire program is a very important part of teaching. Therefore, it is necessary for student participants to examine curriculum guides designed by the district, county, or state (as discussed in chapter 2) so that they can begin to understand how their lessons fit into the entire curriculum. Likewise, it is essential that student participants work with classroom teachers in developing lesson plans, so that the teacher can help them understand this sequence of objectives, goals, lessons, and units. A unit plan format (34A) is provided at the end of this book.

6

TEACHING

TEACHING

Your initial teaching experiences should be successful ones. To ensure their success you should plan carefully and begin slowly. A good place to begin is working with a single student. The first session should be devoted to getting to know the student and letting the student get to know you. Your objective for that session might be simply, "The learner will discuss something about himself or herself with the tutor."

Most student participants are nervous when they face a student or a class for the first time. These jitters are normal, but once you get started, the plan you have developed should give you increasing confidence. To ensure that your plan will be successful, discuss it with the classroom teacher prior to implementing it.

Try to begin each new teaching experience with something you enjoy. For example, you might spend an early session reading and discussing a story you love. Of course, you must be sure that the story is appropriate for the age, interest, and ability of the student(s) with whom you are working. Or, you might do part of a lesson in which you discuss a trip you took. If the fifth grade social studies class is studying Mexico and you recently visited Mexico, for example, your first short lesson plan might include some Mexican music, a few slides you took, sharing a Mexican story, discussing Mexican food, etc.

SAMPLE FORM 35

INSTRUCTIONAL RECORD FORM

Student Participant: <u>Linda Valentine</u>

Date: <u>Feb. 19, 19—</u>

Grade Level/Subject Area: <u>First grade/mathematics</u>

Lesson Taught (Include length, group size, and reason for teaching it): <u>1:15 - 2:00, 2</u>
<u>groups (14, 14). To introduce fractions and how their parts make a whole.</u>

Objective: <u>To assess my successes and concerns about teaching mathematics, and to</u>
<u>determine students' motivation and interest in fractions.</u>

Instructions to Participant: Please select one lesson each week upon which you wish to
reflect. Use the following six questions to guide your thinking. Take as much space as
you need to respond to each question.

1. What did I do? (Type of lesson and procedure used)

*Introduced fractions. Children cut out circles that represent $1/2$, $1/3$, $1/4$. Then I associated each
fraction with something familiar to each child (cake, pizza), separated, and put the fractional parts
back together.*

2. What worked? Why did it work?

Developing a concept that the children could relate to helped the lesson.

3. What were the problems? Why did they occur?

*Keeping all the children on task, asking them to speak when spoken to. The problems might have
occurred due to their level of excitement when they knew the right answer.*

4. What questions do I have about my lesson (e.g., planning, instruction)?

*How do I divide my time evenly among the two groups of students and still have time to offer
extra help?*

5. What did I learn about this instructional strategy? About teaching this content? About this age child?

The success of the lesson depends on the way the lesson is presented.

6. What concerns do I have about teaching <u>first</u> grade?

Maintaining an equal balance of learning activities that are on the level of all of the students.

From: Shirley Raines and Joan Isenberg, Research Roundtable: Reflective Practice. *Journal of Early Childhood Teacher Education*, Winter 1991, p. 25.

TUTORING

Tutoring, teaching, or guiding—usually an individual child—is a very important function of the classroom teacher. But unfortunately, little time is available in most large public school classrooms to work with students one to one. Therefore, the student participants who act as tutors are not only developing teaching skills, but are also providing an important service for the classroom teacher and the students they are tutoring.

Types of Tutoring

Two major types of tutoring are (1) short-term and informal, and (2) long-term and planned. Student participants can experience the first kind of tutoring while assisting the teacher. For example, as pupils are working on writing creative stories, the student participants wander around the classroom, bend down to the eye level of the children, read their stories, make comments, and ask questions. This is informal, short-term tutoring. The kind we will emphasize in this chapter, however, requires planning.

Tutoring that requires planning includes teaching skills in language, mathematics, social studies, science, computers, art, music, health, physical education, etc. Usually, though not always, this tutoring is done with pupils who are experiencing difficulty learning the skill or have missed class skills lessons due to absence.

Tutoring may also involve diagnosing specific strengths and weaknesses. For example, as the pupil reads aloud to the tutor, the tutor might be looking for specific reading problems. Sometimes tutoring is used to remedy these weaknesses. A kindergarten teacher might notice that one student is unable to hold his scissors and cut a simple outline. The teacher has noticed other problems in this child's motor skills when the child is doing physical activities. Since the teacher suspects problems in eye-hand coordination, the tutor will select activities that will help the child develop these skills.

Sometimes tutoring is used to give certain students individual attention. A student may have special needs requiring attention; she or he may be experiencing home problems, or may have a special talent which is not encouraged during the regular class. She or he may be disabled, or the teacher may simply feel the child has been neglected because so many other pupils require special attention. To help you determine tutoring activities in which you can be involved, a checklist is provided below.

SAMPLE FORM 36

CHECKLIST OF TUTORING ACTIVITIES

Name of Student Participant: Nicholas Rapparlie

Name of Pupil(s) Tutored (if appropriate): Frank Mozolic

Name of Teacher: Mr. Sulinski

Grade Level/Subject Area: 4th - Reading/Language Arts/Math

Date: 9/6/19— to 10/30/19—

Objective: To develop teaching skills and to determine students' interests.

Instructions to Student Participant: Listed below are several types of short-term and long-term tutoring activities in which you can participate. As you complete these activities, indicate the date each is accomplished. At the end of each section, there is space for your comments about what you learned from the tutoring activities. Please have the classroom teacher sign this form when your tutoring activities have been completed.

Short-Term, Informal Tutoring Activities	Date Completed
1. Ask individual students questions about something they are reading or writing, a picture they are drawing, or a project they are working on.	9-17
2. Discuss with individual students stories they have read.	9-19
3. Help students with their seat work.	9-6
4. Answer questions students have about their individual work.	9-23

Comment on what you learned from these activities:
I learned that fourth graders seem to forget a lot over the summer. Some needed help with easy words like "master," and some needed help with simple multiplication. Many liked to draw about outer space and tell me about their Nintendo games. A few liked to read stories about racing cars and Antarctica.

Long-Term, Planned Tutoring Activities	Date Completed
1. Teaching skills that have not been mastered by individual students (e.g., grammar, composition, reading, mathematical computations, times tables, word problems, word processing, using a computer program, using a table of contents, reading a textbook for meaning, cutting out objects, using a microscope, etc.) List the skill(s) you taught:	10-22

Syllabication—dividing between 2 syllables; after prefixes and before suffixes.

| 2. Diagnosing a student's strength or weakness (e.g., administering a specific individual test, listening to a student read, asking a student questions on a variety of levels, watching a student do a mathematical computation, observing a student using a computer program, watching a student use a piece of equipment, etc.). List the method(s) you employed and what you were attempting to diagnose: | 9-27 |

Had student read 6 passages from grade levels 1–6 silently, then had student respond to 5 questions of varied levels of difficulty after each passage. I wanted to determine the student's comprehension level. It was 5th grade.

| 3. Remedying a weakness (e.g., helping a student learn to cut out a shape with scissors, assisting a student with rules of phonics or grammar, drilling a student on vocabulary, showing a student how to find meaning in a paragraph, demonstrating for a student how to use a piece of equipment safely, etc.). List the method(s) you employed and the weakness you were attempting to remedy: | 10-30 |

—listed Halloween words for student to divide into syllables and use those words to write a Halloween story.
—Wanted to determine if student could apply syllabication rules.

| 4. Developing a special talent (e.g., teaching the student a technique of drawing, reading a piece of student writing and providing support and suggestions, listening to a student read and discussing what has been read, talking to a student about a historical event, working with a student on a science project, helping a student complete a woodworking project, teaching basic computer programming, taking the student to a museum, etc.). List the method(s) you employed and the talent you were attempting to develop: | 9-11 |

Wanted to motivate student to read about current events from newspapers/journals, not just hear it on T.V. We read reports of Desert Storm, hoping this would motivate him to read further.

| 5. Other (List specific long-range tutoring activities in which you have participated): | 10-17 |

Helped student do research on deserts. Student needed a lot of help finding and using a variety of reference/media material. He did write a good outline and a fairly good paper.

Comment on what you learned from these activities:
Students at this age need to practice library skills and use them in their writing.

I certify that the student participant listed above has successfully completed those tutoring activities indicated above.

Mr. Sulinski
_____
(Classroom Teacher's Signature)

Planning for Tutoring

So that the tutoring is as valuable as possible to the tutor as well as the pupil, it is essential that careful planning be done prior to every session. The student participant should discuss with the classroom teacher the specific goals for the tutoring sessions. The tutor should then check the district, county, or state curriculum guides to determine where these goals fit in with the sequence of goals to be accomplished during the school year. Then the tutor should set specific objectives for each tutoring session.

For example, if the teacher's goal is to provide a child with more practice in reading aloud, the tutor checks the state curriculum guide and finds the following related goals: the learner will (1) demonstrate adequacy of *oral expression,* (2) demonstrate adequacy of *auditory discrimination* and *memory,* (3) develop *oral vocabulary,* and (4) demonstrate adequate *comprehension skills.* In addition, the tutor discovers many goals in the areas of phonics and comprehension that might relate to the pupil's oral reading.

The tutor decides to begin with those goals directly related to reading aloud. Therefore, after a well-planned introductory session in which the tutor and pupil talk about themselves, the tutor begins the next session by asking the pupil to pick one of three stories she would like the tutor to read to her. Her selection might tell the tutor some things about the child with whom he is working. The tutor reads the story to her, stopping at appropriate points to discuss it. After they have completed the story, the tutor asks several questions about the story, mentally noting areas of weakness in aural (listening) comprehension. Next the tutor asks the pupil to read the story to him. He hopes that she will find this less threatening than reading a new story, since the story is already familiar to her. As the child reads, the tutor looks for specific problems she is experiencing. Immediately following the session, the tutor makes a list of these problems, discusses them with the classroom teacher, and uses them as the basis for some subsequent sessions. Below is a checklist you can use as you plan for tutoring.

SAMPLE FORM 37

TUTORING PLANNING CHECKLIST

Name of Student Participant: <u>Agnes Rowan</u>

Name of Pupil(s) Tutored: <u>Frank Delaney</u>

Name of Teacher: <u>Mrs. Numata</u>

Grade Level/Subject Area: <u>6th grade</u>

Date: <u>September 25, 19—</u>

Objective: <u>To develop teaching skills: diagnosing, planning, finding materials, confer-</u>
<u>ring, evaluating with teacher.</u>

Instructions to Tutor: As you complete each of the following in your tutoring plans,
indicate the date completed.

Planning Activity	Date Completed
1. Discuss the student you will tutor with the classroom teacher.	9-26
2. Discuss possible tutoring topics and technqiues with the classroom teacher.	9-26
3. Carefully plan an initial "getting-to-know-you" session with the student.	9-27
4. Diagnose student strengths and weaknesses as necessary.	9-30
5. Check available curriculum guides to determine skills to be taught and their sequence.	10-2
6. Set a specific objective for each tutoring session.	10-3 and 4
7. Develop a plan for each small-group session (appropriate plan formats can be found on pp. 148, 150, and 151, and in chapter 5, pp. 77–79).	Began 10-7 to 11-15
8. Consult appropriate resources for teaching techniques and materials.	10-7 to 11-15
9. Make sure all necessary materials are available and copied prior to each tutoring session.	10-7 to 11-15
10. Monitor the pupil's progress by keeping a log of each day's tutoring.	10-7 to 11-15
11. Discuss student's progress with the classroom teacher. Ask for additional suggestions for helping the student.	10-9, 10-16, 10-29

The basic elements of a tutoring lesson are the same as the elements of a
lesson taught to a class. The tutor must: (1) get the attention and interest of the
pupil; (2) relate the objective for the session; (3) attempt to determine prerequisite learning, ask questions, and fill in gaps; (4) guide the student through what

is expected, model the learning to be accomplished; (5) allow the student to attempt the skill/concept on his/her own; (6) provide feedback; (7) tie together the lesson by discussing what has been learned, what the pupil needs to do next, and what will be done in the next tutoring session. In addition, each session should provide some means of assessing the pupil's progress. These steps are roughly parallel to the steps in a lesson plan (see pp. 148, 150, and 151, and in chapter 5, pp. 77–79) for an entire class and can be used, with limited modifications, for any type of tutoring.

SMALL GROUPS

After student participants have worked successfully with one student in a tutoring situation, they may direct their teaching to a small group of students. Frequently, small groups of students work together without direct instruction to complete a task. However, the small group we will emphasize is an instructional small group, similar in many respects to the tutorial teaching situation discussed above. In fact, small-group instruction is frequently called multi-student tutoring.

Purpose of Small Groups

Penny Ur, in her book *Discussions that Work* (1981), points out many of the advantages of small-group work, the first being increased participation by the students. In a classroom of thirty, each individual can respond for a maximum of only one minute during a thirty-minute lesson, and this assumes that the entire lesson involves student response. By contrast, in a group of five, each individual can respond for six minutes during the same thirty-minute period. Moreover, according to Ur, this heightened participation not only includes those who are articulate and frequently participate, but also those who are shy and rarely say anything in front of the entire class.

Second, according to Ur, the motivation of participants improves as they work in small groups. This is partly due to reduced inhibition, but it also occurs because group work frequently focuses on the individuals within the group, whereas whole-class work rarely focuses on the individual. The group is more personal, and participants are therefore more likely to want to be involved.

Small-group work lends itself to more active learning such as games, activities, learning centers, experiments, simulations, discussions, etc. Group work, according to Ur, tends to be task-centered, and since students retain more from active rather than receptive instruction, small groups are likely to encourage more learning.

Group work can free the teacher from the role of instructor and controller. When students are working in small groups, the teacher can move about the room, helping students when necessary and focusing attention on those students most in need of assistance.

Group work can allow for peer-teaching, making the teaching and learning that occurs in the classroom far more efficient than in the large-group situation. For example, if all students play the role of teacher as well as learner, the amount of teaching is significantly increased. In addition, there is more variety in techniques of teaching than when only one teacher instructs.

Many educators, such as Gene Stanford in *Developing Effective Classroom Groups* (1977), believe that small-group work encourages more abstract levels of thought than does traditional, receptive learning. This is because group members analyze and evaluate each other's contributions to solutions of problems and synthesize various contributions into a final group product.

Additionally, small-group work provides a planned structure for implementing democratic education without much permissiveness, according to Shlomo Sharan and Yael Sharan in *Small Group Teaching* (1976). Student members of small groups are frequently involved in the decision-making process. They might select from several possible activities or various approaches to a single problem. Likewise, student members of groups select peers to take leadership roles. Frequently, groups have elected chairpersons and recorders. Or, at times, these leadership positions arise naturally from the needs of the group.

James Moffet and Betty Jane Wagner in *Student-Centered Language Arts and Reading* (1983) contend that one of the most important reasons for small-group work is that it allows students to communicate with each other, which is important in developing language skills. Group work allows for constructive classroom student talk.

Functions of Small Groups

Small groups can have a variety of functions. They can facilitate learning by allowing students to work together on a skill that all members are having difficulty mastering. Each group might be assigned to read a different story or book. For example, all students who are reading one to two years below grade level may be grouped together for that subject. Individual groups may be working on an assigned or chosen research project, depending on their abilities or interests.

Brainstorming and/or discussion may be the objective of a small group in order to develop creativity or rational thinking skills. A group may work on a simulation game or in a play area in a preschool or elementary school classroom. A group may be randomly assigned to complete a specified activity or to serve a management or class government function. For example, they may plan a class trip or clean up the playground. Or, the group may be long-term, with students helping each other with specific skills such as writing or understanding fractions.

Structure of Small Groups

The structure of any group varies according to its function. Frequently, small groups involve students working independently of the teacher on a project arising from classroom work. At other times, groups may work with the teacher for a short period of time while the task or assignment is explained or guidance is given, and then work independently. Or the teacher may instruct one small group while other students in the class work without the teacher's immediate guidance.

Small-Group Instruction

Since classroom teachers frequently recognize a need to instruct small groups of students but have only limited time to do so, student participants can meet an instructional need by assuming the responsibility for one small group. In an instructional group, the teacher's guidance is required to assist the students in completing their task. Therefore, the small-group instruction designed by the student participant should be work that the students are unlikely to be able to complete successfully without instruction.

Planning for Small-Group Teaching

The sequence of the lesson plan is nearly the same as in tutoring, but in this case several students are involved in the learning. Therefore, the student participant must consider the needs and abilities of all group members and must develop assessment instruments that can measure the progress of several students simultaneously.

SAMPLE FORM 38

PRE-PLANNING SMALL GROUP CHECKLIST

Name of Student Participant: Maria Ramos

Name of Teacher: Mrs. Little

Grade Level/Subject Area: Fifth grade/Math

Date: Sept./Oct. 19—

Objective: To practice my teaching skills in a small group and to determine students' motivation.

Instructions to Student Participant: As you complete each of the following in planning for your small group, indicate the date completed.

Pre-planning Activity	Date Completed
1. Discuss possible types of small-group teaching with the classroom teacher.	9-13
2. Discuss the assignment of students to the small group.	9-13
3. Discuss the classroom teacher's goal for the small group.	9-13
4. Consider the needs, interests, and abilities of the students who will participate in the instructional group. Discuss with the classroom teacher.	9-16

5. Develop an assessment tool or technique that can measure the progress of several students simultaneously (e.g., students complete mathematics problems that begin slightly below their level of achievement and continue beyond their level of achievement; students answer questions about reading samples that are below their reading level and continue beyond their reading level; students complete multiple-choice items on a leveled vocabulary list; students attempt to perform part of a one-act play; students read parts orally in a short play; etc.).   9-18

6. Determine a specific objective for each small-group session.   9-19

7. Develop a plan for each tutoring session (appropriate plan formats can be found on pp. 148, 150, and 151, and in chapter 5, pp. 77–79).   Began 9-23 to
                                                       10-11

8. Consult appropriate resources for teaching techniques and materials.   9-24

9. Make sure all necessary materials are available and copied prior to each small-group session.   9-23 to 10-11

10. Monitor the pupils' progress by having them complete individual practice exercises related to each session's objective.   9-23 to 10-11

11. Discuss the students' progress with the classroom teacher. Ask for additional suggesitons for helping the students.   9-24
                                                       9-27
                                                       10-28

The student participant must be sure that all students in the group possess prerequisite knowledge for learning the concepts or skills to be taught. For example, if the students are grouped together to find the least common denominator, each student must already possess the prerequisite concepts of numerator, denominator, factor, and multiple, as well as knowing how to multiply and divide small whole numbers and how to add fractions with identical denominators. Therefore, an important part of planning for small-group instruction is determining each student's level of prerequisite knowledge.

To determine if students possess prerequisite skills and knowledge, you might want to begin the lesson, after you have gained the students' attention and explained the objective of the group work, with a task you are sure group members can accomplish. For example, the small group has been assigned to complete research on the Civil War from the perspective of various groups of Southerners (for example, plantation owners, small planters, merchants, government officials, slaves). In order to accomplish this task, students will need to possess some basic research skills. Therefore, you decide to teach the lesson in the library. Early in the lesson each student is required to find a reference book or article in a maximum of five minutes. If one or more of the students has problems finding the reference materials, you and the group members might discuss the problem. If most of the members seem unable to accomplish the task, you might decide to teach library skills, or to obtain for the students the reference material needed to complete the research. If the classroom teacher's goal is for the group to complete the research within a short period of time, the student participant, with the help of the librarian, might locate the materials for the students and report to the classroom teacher the students' apparent weakness in library skills. A checklist of activities for small-group lessons follows.

SAMPLE FORM 39

SMALL-GROUP TEACHING CHECKLIST

Name of Student Participant: <u>Loretta Connor</u>

Name of Teacher: <u>Mr. Lebowitz</u>

Grade Level/Subject Area: <u>9th grade/History</u>

Topic: <u>The Constitution</u>

Date: <u>Nov. 20, 19—</u>

Objective: <u>To implement a well-planned lesson; practice teaching skills.</u>

Instructions to Student Participant: Use this checklist as you prepare to teach and during your teaching of your small group. To be sure that your lesson includes each of the following, check each item off as it occurs.

Teaching Activity	Appears in Lesson
1. The students' attention is grabbed.	✔
2. The objective of the lesson is related to the students.	✔
3. Prerequisite knowledge is ascertained through questions and answers, a quiz, completion of an exercise, etc.	✔
4. If appropriate, gaps in needed information are filled in.	✔
5. New information, skills, or materials are presented through explanation, demonstration, discussion, etc.	✔
6. Individual tasks are assigned each group member.	N/A
7. Student performance is elicited and monitored through independent work.	✔
8. Teacher feedback is provided to each student.	✔
9. Student work is related to previous and future learning.	✔
10. Students review what they have learned in the lesson.	✔
11. The objective for the next small-group lesson is determined and communicated to the students.	✔

Although the small-group instructor must remain flexible to meet the needs and abilities of the students, a well-planned lesson is essential. Without careful planning, little or inadequate learning is likely to occur. For example, if you were a student participant working with the Civil War activity described above and had not carefully planned the group work, you might stray from the objective—"the students will examine the Civil War from the perspective of various groups of Southerners"—to teach skills that students don't really need to complete the assignment. Although library skills are essential if the students are to find their own references, they are not required if the references are located for the students by the teacher and librarian.

LARGE GROUPS

After student participants have successfully instructed individual students and small groups of students, they are ready to work with a large group or the entire class. Due to the variety of individuals in a large group of twenty or more students, instruction is not as precise as with individuals and small groups. Learning theorist Robert Gagne in *The Principles of Instructional Design* (1979) refers to the teacher's amount of control over instructional events as the "degree of precision" (p. 258). According to Gagne, precision decreases as numbers of students in the instructional group grow. This lack of precision occurs because each student in the large group learns differently, possesses varied prerequisite knowledge, has had different experiences, works at different skill levels, has had varied instructional experiences and successes, possesses differing attitudes about education, has different interests and needs, etc. To increase the teacher's control over classroom events, careful planning that addresses student differences is required.

Getting Started

The more prepared you are to teach a large-group lesson, the less nervous you are likely to be. Feeling confident comes from feeling prepared for the material to be presented; knowing the students through observation, tutoring, and small-group work; having planned well; and having shared and discussed those plans with the classroom teacher and your university instructor.

An excellent way to get started is to plan to teach a lesson (or parts of a lesson) on a concept or skill that is particularly familiar to you. For example, if you have spent a semester in Great Britain, a lesson introducing students to the country through slides, music, oral reading, and discussion can be a good initial lesson. The students have an opportunity to learn something about you, their new teacher, and your first teaching experience is likely to be more rewarding since you are so comfortable with the material.

Planning for the Large Group

Many components of the large-group lesson plan are almost identical to the tutoring and small-group plans. However, the large-group plan must recognize the wide variety of learners in the classroom. Here are some steps in the large-group plan.

(1) *Gaining the attention of the learner* is even more important in large-group instruction than in tutoring or small-group instruction, since lack of attention by one or more students in the large group can lead to serious discipline problems. There are many ways to gain the attention of students. Demonstrations, oral readings, audiovisual presentations, provocative questions, and dramatic monologues are a few commonly used techniques.

(2) *Informing students of the lesson's objective(s)* gives the learners a sense of direction and a common goal.

(3) *Stimulating recall of prerequisite learning* is of critical importance, but it is very difficult to do successfully in a large group. Although no approach to helping students recall previous learning can be successful with all students, you can help by reviewing material covered in the previous class, asking students probing questions, having students complete short activities or exercises, requiring students to review their notes early in the class period and frame questions or write a summarizing paragraph based on their notes, reviewing homework assignments from previous classes, etc.

(4) *Presenting the new material to be learned* should emphasize, according to Robert Gagne, distinctive features of the new concept or skill (1979, p. 254). For example, if the students have been working in the library to develop research skills and have just completed using the card catalog to locate books on a particular topic, the new lesson might involve using the *Guide to Periodical Literature* to discover information about their topic.

(5) The student participant must *provide learning guidance* using a variety of techniques to assist all kinds of learners. For example, if the new concept deals with a historic event, you can help students understand this event by showing pictures (still or motion) of it, placing it on a class-constructed timeline, having the students research various aspects of the event, conducting a simulation of the event, having small groups prepare dramatic episodes, orally reading eyewitness accounts of the event, etc. The more learners use all their senses in dealing with a new skill or concept, the more likely they are to retain it. The use of all the senses requires active participation by each learner during a significant part of every lesson.

(6) So that learners know if they are reaching the objective, you should *provide feedback* in each lesson. This can be done through quizzes, student board work, exercises, activities, tests, assignments, question and answer sessions, oral reports given by small groups or individuals, brief student/teacher conferences (these can be as short as a few seconds as the teacher circulates throughout the room commenting on each student's work), etc.

(7) The student participant must assist the learner in *retention and transfer* of concepts and skills. This can be done through reviews; having students summarize the major concepts of the lesson in a journal (précis writing); teaching the students to take notes and requiring them to do so; adding the material covered in the lesson to a timeline, chart, or graph, etc.

Below is a checklist of additional helpful hints for teaching large groups of students.

SAMPLE FORM 40

SAMPLE CHECKLIST FOR WORKING WITH LARGE GROUPS

Name of Student Participant: Amy Poulimenos

Name of Teacher: Mrs. Garner

Grade Level/Subject Area: 11th/Biology

Date: 10/17/19—

Objective: To practice my teaching/management skills with a large group.

Instructions to Student Participant: As you complete each of these activities, check it off in the right-hand column.

Activity	Completed
Management of the Classroom	
1. Discuss management rules with the classroom teacher.	✔
2. Ascertain consequences for infractions with the classroom teacher.	✔
3. Use only the discipline methods sanctioned by the classroom teacher and the school.	✔
4. Communicate the rules and consequences to the students so that they know you will enforce them.	✔
5. Enforce rules and apply consequences consistently.	didn't work one time
6. Do not threaten if you do not intend to carry through on the threat (e.g., "If you aren't quiet, I'll keep you all after school").	✔
7. Make eye contact with as many students as possible.	✔
8. Call students by name. (Make a temporary seating chart to help you learn names or have the students make, wear, or display name tags.)	(did) ✔
Teaching	
1. Carefully plan lessons and divide them into clear segments (use a planning format such as those provided on pp. 148, 150, and 151, and in chapter 5, pp. 77–79).	✔
2. Be sure all materials are copied and ready to distribute.	✔
3. Preview all materials prior to using or showing.	✔
4. Preread anything you intend to use.	✔
5. Maintain instructional momentum (keep up the pace; do not spend too long on any one element of the plan; do not over-explain).	✔
6. Be certain that students understand what is expected (e.g., ask them to explain to you what they are to do; place assignments on the chalkboard prior to the lesson; make sure instructions and printing on handouts are clear; provide clear examples).	✔

7. Be sure students know how to and are capable of accomplishing the task (e.g., beware of asking students to do tasks for which they do not have prerequisite knowledge or skills; check with the classroom teacher to be sure they will be able to accomplish what you expect).   ✔

8. Review previous lessons and prerequisite knowledge or skills required for this lesson.   ✔

9. Actively involve the students in the lesson.   ✔

10. Use teaching methodology appropriate to the subject and the maturity of the students (e.g., labs in science classes, oral reading and independent writing in English and language arts, problem solving in mathematics, research in social studies, etc.).   Tried, the teacher said I did

11. Employ a variety of teaching techniques so that all types of learners can achieve (e.g., audiovisuals, hands-on activities, problem solving, student-designed charts and graphs, laboratories, demonstrations, etc.).   ✔

12. Assess students' level of mastery of skills and concepts as often as possible (e.g., class work that requires demonstration of mastery, observation of students completing classwork, homework that is not merely drill, quizzes, journal entries, writing assignments, etc.   ✔

13. Expect mastery of skills and concepts after a period of teaching, practice, coaching, assessing, reteaching, practice, coaching, etc.   N/A

14. Do not expect all students to master all concepts and skills in the same way or at the same time. Group students to provide additional assistance to those who have not mastered important concepts and skills. Use different teaching techniques with these students, or allow those who have mastered the skills or concepts to tutor those who have not.   ✔

After teaching the lesson, you might want to reflect on what was successful and what was less than successful. To help you do this, we have provided an instructional record form 35A like the one completed by Linda Valentine in the sample instructional record form (sample 35 on p. 82).

PART III

Forms

FORM 1A

ANECDOTAL RECORD FORM FOR
OBSERVING TEACHERS OR INSTRUCTIONAL EVENTS—1

Name of Observer: _____

Date and Time of Observation: _____

Length of Observation: _____

Person and/or Event Observed: _____

Grade Level and/or Subject: _____

Objective of Observation: _____

_____

Instructions to the Observer: As completely and accurately as possible, describe the person or the event. If appropriate, include direct quotes and descriptions of the location or individual. Try to avoid making judgments.

FORM 2A

ANECDOTAL TEACHER-STUDENT INTERACTION FORM

Name of Observer: _____

Date and Time of Observation: _____

Length of Observation: _____

Name of Teacher: _____

Name of Student: _____

Grade Level and/or Subject: _____

Objective of Observation: _____

_____

Instructions to the Observer: As completely and accurately as possible, describe the interactions between the teacher and one selected student. Include direct quotes and descriptions of the teacher and the student, including facial expressions, gestures, and voice quality. However, be careful to avoid making judgments.

Time	Teacher	Student

FORM 3A

ANECDOTAL RECORD FORM FOR OBSERVING TEACHERS OR INSTRUCTIONAL EVENTS—2

Name of Observer: _____

Date and Time of Observation: _____

Length of Observation: _____

Person and/or Event Observed: _____

Grade Level and/or Subject: _____

Objective of Observation: _____

_____

Instructions to the Observer: As completely and accurately as possible, describe the person or the event. If appropriate, include direct quotes and descriptions of the location or the individual. Try to avoid making judgments.

FORM 4A

ANECDOTAL RECORD FORM FOR GROUPING PATTERNS

Name of Observer: _____

Date and Time of Observation: _____

Length of Observation: _____

Person and/or Event Observed: _____

Grade Level and/or Subject: _____

Objective of Observation: _____

_____

Instructions to the Observer: As completely and accurately as possible, describe the patterns. If appropriate, include direct quotes and descriptions of locations or individuals. Try to avoid making judgments.

FORM 5A

OBSERVATION FORM FOR RANK ORDERING

Name of Observer: _____

Date and Time of Observation: _____

Length of Observation: _____

Techniques or Types Observed: _____

Grade Level and/or Subject: _____

Objective of Observation: _____

Instructions to the Observer: You will need to know a variety of possible techniques or types. Keep a tally of those you observe. At the end of the observation period, count the number of occurrences of each technique or type.

Techniques or Types:	Number of Occurrences

FORM 6A

CODING SYSTEM FORM I—STUDENT-TEACHER INTERACTION DURING SPECIFIED INTERVALS

Name of Observer: _____

Date and Time of Observation: _____

Length of Observation: _____

Intervals at Which Behavior Is Recorded: _____

Element Observed: _____

Teacher and/or Student: _____

Grade Level and/or Subject: _____

Objective of Observation: _____

_____

Instructions to the Observer: After each interval, record the instance you have observed. Identify the people whose behavior you are observing, and specifically describe their behavior. If possible, use direct quotes. Finally, indicate the code number of the instance you have observed from the codes listed on pages 9 and 10.

Name	Behavior	Code

FORM 7A

CODING SYSTEM FORM II—TYPE AND TALLY OF STUDENT-TEACHER INTERACTION

Name of Observer: _____

Date and Time of Observation: _____

Length of Observation: _____

Element Observed: _____

Teacher and/or Student: _____

Grade Level and/or Subject: _____

Objective of Observation: _____

_____

Instructions to the Observer: Tally the number of times each interactive behavior occurs during your observation period. Try to record at least one example of each type of interaction. At the end of the observation period, total the number of all teacher-student interactions and calculate the percentage of the total for each interaction.

Type of Interactive Behavior	Tally of Times Observed	Percentage
INDIRECT		
Accepts Feelings: Example:		
Praises/Encourages: Example:		
Accepts or Uses Student Ideas: Example:		

Asks Questions:
  Example:

DIRECT
Lectures:
  Example:

Gives Directions:
  Example:

Criticizes or Justifies Authority:
  Example:

STUDENT TALK
Student Talk-Response:
  Example:

Student Talk-Initiation:
  Example:

The type of interaction most frequently used:

Adapted from Ned Flanders, 1985.

FORM 8A

OBSERVATION FORM FOR
EXAMINING QUESTIONS

Name of Observer: _____

Date and Time of Observation: _____

Teacher: _____

Grade Level and/or Subject: _____

Objective of Observation: _____

_____

Instructions to the Observer: On a separate piece of paper or on a cassette record all questions asked by the teacher, orally and in writing, for one lesson. Then place each question below at the appropriate level. Next, tally the number of questions at each level. Count the total number of questions asked, and compute a percentage for each level.

1. Memory:

Total # of Memory Questions:

2. Translation:

Total # of Translation Questions:

3. Intepretation:

Total # of Interpretation Questions:

4. Application:

Total # of Application Questions:

5. Analysis:

Total # of Analysis Questions:

6. Synthesis:

Total # of Synthesis Questions:

7. Evaluation:

Total # of Evaluation Questions:

Total # of Questions, All Levels:

Percentage of Memory   ; Translation   ; Interpretation   ; Application   ;
Analysis   ; Synthesis   ; Evaluation   .

FORM 9A

CHECKLIST FOR AUTHORITARIAN MANAGEMENT MODEL

Name of Observer: _____

Date and Time of Observation: _____

Length of Observation: _____

Teacher: _____

Grade Level and/or Subject: _____

Objective of Observation: _____

_____

Instructions to the Observer: Prior to the observation, read over the items on the authoritarian management model checklist. These represent the elements that should be present in classrooms in which authoritarian management is used. During and after the observation, place a check next to those elements you have observed.

_____ Students understand the teacher's expectations and act accordingly.

_____ Students exhibit productive work and study behaviors.

_____ Students understand and adhere to school and classroom rules.

_____ Students evidence feelings of self-worth.

_____ Students feel free to express themselves to the teacher and to one another.

_____ Students follow clearly established routines.

_____ Students show respect for persons and property.

_____ Students communicate openly and honestly.

_____ Students manifest positive interpersonal relationships.

_____ Students feel accountable for their own behavior.

_____ Students exhibit group cohesiveness.

_____ Students understand and accept the consequences of their actions.

_____ Students feel that they are treated fairly.

_____ Students exhibit cooperativeness and a sharing attitude.

_____ Students display productive group norms.

_____ Students quickly return to task after interruptions.

_____ Students follow directions.

_____ Students are prepared for the task at hand.

_____ Students function at a noise level appropriate to the activity.

_____ Students participate actively in learning tasks.

_____ Students display positive feelings about classroom processes.

_____ Students manifest the ability to adjust to changing situations.

_____ Students exhibit self-discipline and self-control.

_____ Students feel comfortable and safe.

_____ Students display initiative and creativity.

_____ Students serve as resources to one another.

_____ Students move from one task to another in an orderly manner.

_____ Students accept and respect authority.

_____ Students support and encourage one another.

_____ Students are responsible for individual supplies and materials.

_____ Students pay attention to the teacher and to one another.

_____ Students like being members of the classroom group.

_____ Students feel that the teacher understands them.

_____ Students believe that they have opportunities to be successful.

Checklist items based on the work of Wilford A. Weber, _Classroom Management_, 1982, pp. 289–290.

FORM 10A

FORM FOR STRUCTURED OBSERVATION
OF A LESSON

Name of Observer: _____

Date and Time of Observation: _____

Teacher: _____

Grade Level and/or Subject: _____

Objective of Observation: _____

_____

Instructions to the Observer: As you observe in the classroom, list the elements of the lesson under the categories below. A description of each category appears in italics.

(1) **Anticipatory Set** - *In every lesson the teacher provides initial motivation and focus for the lesson. Sometimes this focus takes the form of a review of previous knowledge important to this lesson; at other times it is designed to "grab" the students' attention. Key words: alerting, relevance, relationship (to previous lesson), meaningfulness, etc.*

(2) **Objective** - *In almost every lesson the teacher specifies the behaviors the students will be expected to perform. In other words, the student knows what is expected of him/her and what s/he is expected to learn.*

(3) **Teacher Input** - *In most lessons the teacher will provide the student with the information needed to reach the objective successfully. Sometimes the teacher will show the student how to accomplish the task by modeling appropriate performance.*

(4) **Checking for Understanding** - *Throughout the lesson the teacher checks to ensure that the students understand the concepts or skills being taught. This can be accomplished through random questioning or individual tutoring.*

(5) **Guided Practice** - *In every lesson the student practices the expected performance. This may include exercises completed with the teacher, examples done by students on the board, students reading aloud, students working together to complete assignments, games that allow the students to exhibit understanding, etc.*

(6) **Independent Practice** - *The student independently exhibits the behaviors set forth in the objective. To accomplish this, the student might complete problems, write a paper, do an experiment, give a report, complete a project, do research, etc.*

(7) **Closure** - *The teacher helps the student review what s/he has learned in the lesson. This may include a summary of the lesson, questions about what happened during the student's independent practice, the students' report of their progress, an evaluation by the teacher, relationship of this lesson to the next lesson or the unit, assignment of additional independent practice.*

Adapted from: Lois Sprinthall, *A Strategy Guide for Teachers: Guide Book for Supervisors of Novice Teachers.* Unpublished manuscript.

FORM 11A

CHECKLIST OF INTERVIEWING TECHNIQUES

Name of Observer: _____

Date and Time of Observation: _____

Person to Be Interviewed: _____

Grade Level and/or Subject: _____

Objective of Observation: _____

_____

Instructions to the Observer: Review this checklist prior to and after your interview. Check off items you have completed.

Prior to the Interview

_____ Establish a purpose of the interview.

_____ Request an appointment (time and place) giving sufficient lead time for you and the person to be interviewed.

_____ Plan objective, specific questions related to the purpose of the interview.

_____ Prioritize questions, asking the most important first.

_____ Remind the person to be interviewed of the time, place, and purpose of the interview.

The Interview

_____ Arrive at preestablished place several minutes before the scheduled time for the interview.

_____ Start the interview by reminding the person to be interviewed of the purpose of the interview.

_____ Request permission to tape the interview (if appropriate).

_____ If unable to tape, take careful, objective notes trying to list direct quotes as often as possible.

_____ Avoid inserting impressions or judgments.

_____ Limit the interview to no more than 15–30 minutes.

After the Interview

_____ Review with the respondent what has been said or heard.

_____ Express your appreciation for the interview.

_____ Offer to share the interview report with the respondent.

FORM 12A

FORM FOR ANECDOTAL RECORD
OF CLASSROOM ORGANIZATION

Name of Observer: _____

Date and Time of Observation: _____

Length of Observation: _____

Person and/or Event Observed: _____

Grade Level and/or Subject: _____

Objective of Observation: _____

_____

Instructions to the Observer: As completely and accurately as possible, describe the organization of the classroom. Be sure to include as much detail as possible. Try to avoid making judgments.

FORM 13A

FORM FOR A CLASSROOM MAP

Name of Observer: _____

Date and Time of Observation: _____

Person and/or Event Observed: _____

Grade Level and/or Subject: _____

Objective of Observation: _____

_____

Instructions to the Observer: Draw a map of the classroom you are observing. Include seating arrangements, placement of furniture and other equipment. Then give a brief anecdotal description of these elements of the classroom: lighting, traffic patterns, instructional displays, management, and motivational elements.

Draw classroom map:

Anecdotal discussion of classroom elements:

Lighting and Traffic Patterns:

Instructional Displays, Management and Motivational Elements:

FORM 14A

FORM FOR CODING SCALE
OF CLASSROOM SOCIAL ENVIRONMENT

Name of Observer: _____

Date and Time of Observation: _____

Length of Observation: _____

Person and/or Event Observed: _____

Grade Level and/or Subject: _____

Objective of Observation: _____

_____

Instructions to the Observer: Before using the scale, become familiar with the descriptions of each of the 15 dimensions of a classroom social environment. These descriptions will be found on pp. 28–30. The scale is divided into three sets (numbered 1–15, 16–30, and 31–45). Each item represents one element of one of the 15 dimensions. Every fifteenth item begins a new set of items, following the order of the dimensions in the first set (e.g., numbers 1, 16, and 31 represent one dimension; numbers 2, 17, and 32 another, and so on).

After observing in a classroom, mark the appropriate rating on each item. Note that some of the items are phrased negatively, and the numbers next to these items have been reversed. Average the three elements of each dimension (e.g., numbers 15, 30, and 45). Note that for several of the dimensions being measured (diversity, speed, difficulty, democracy, and competitiveness), a higher score is not necessarily more desirable.

	Strongly Disagree	Disagree	Agree	Strongly Agree	No Information
1. A student in this class has the chance to get to know all other students (cohesiveness).	1	2	3	4	N/I
2. The class has students with many different interests (diversity).	1	2	3	4	N/I
3. There is a set of rules for the students to follow (formality).	1	2	3	4	N/I
4. Most of the class has difficulty keeping up with the assigned work (speed).	1	2	3	4	N/I
5. The books and equipment students need or want are easily available in the classroom (environment).	1	2	3	4	N/I
6. There are tensions among certain students that tend to interfere with class activities (friction).	1	2	3	4	N/I
7. Most students have little idea of what the class is attempting to accomplish (goal direction).	4	3	2	1	N/I
8. The better students' questions are answered more sympathetically than those of the average student (favoritism).	1	2	3	4	N/I
9. Some students refuse to mix with the rest of the class (cliquishness).	1	2	3	4	N/I
10. The students seem to enjoy their classwork (satisfaction).	1	2	3	4	N/I
11. There are long periods during which the class does nothing (disorganization).	1	2	3	4	N/I
12. Some students in the class consider the work difficult (difficulty).	1	2	3	4	N/I
13. Most students seem to have a concern for the progress of the class (apathy).	4	3	2	1	N/I
14. When group discussions occur, all students tend to contribute (democracy).	1	2	3	4	N/I
15. Most students cooperate rather than compete with one another in this class (competitiveness).	4	3	2	1	N/I
16. Students in this class are not in close enough contact to develop likes and dislikes for one another.	4	3	2	1	N/I
17. The class is working toward many different goals.	1	2	3	4	N/I
18. Students who break the rules are penalized.	1	2	3	4	N/I
19. The class has plenty of time to cover the prescribed amount of work.	4	3	2	1	N/I
20. A comprehensive collection of reference material is available in the classroom for students to use.	1	2	3	4	N/I
21. Certain students seem to have no respect for other students.	1	2	3	4	N/I
22. The objectives of the class are not clearly recognized.	4	3	2	1	N/I
23. Every member of the class is given the same privileges.	4	3	2	1	N/I
24. Certain students work only with their close friends.	1	2	3	4	N/I
25. There is considerable student dissatisfaction with the classwork.	4	3	2	1	N/I
26. Classwork is frequently interrupted by some students with nothing to do.	4	3	2	1	N/I
27. Most students in this class are constantly challenged.	1	2	3	4	N/I
28. Some members of the class don't care what the class does.	1	2	3	4	N/I
29. Certain students have more influence on the class than others.	4	3	2	1	N/I
30. Most students in the class want their work to be better than their friends' work.	1	2	3	4	N/I
31. This class is made up of individuals who do not know each other well.	4	3	2	1	N/I
32. Different students are interested in different aspects of the class.	4	3	2	1	N/I
33. There is a right and wrong way of going about class activities.	4	3	2	1	N/I
34. There is little time in this class for daydreaming.	4	3	2	1	N/I
35. There are bulletin board displays and pictures around the room.	4	3	2	1	N/I
36. Certain students in this class are uncooperative.	1	2	3	4	N/I
37. Most of the class realizes exactly how much work is required.	1	2	3	4	N/I
38. Certain students in the class are favored over others.	1	2	3	4	N/I
39. Most students cooperate equally well with all class members.	4	3	2	1	N/I
40. After an assignment, most students have a sense of satisfaction.	1	2	3	4	N/I
41. The class is well organized and efficient.	4	3	2	1	N/I
42. Most students consider the subject matter easy.	4	3	2	1	N/I
43. Students show a common concern for the success of the class.	4	3	2	1	N/I
44. Each member of the class has as much influence as does any other member.	4	3	2	1	N/I
45. Students compete to see who can do the best work.	4	3	2	1	N/I

From: Gary Borich, *Observation Skills for Effective Teaching*, 1990, pp. 113–115.

FORM 15A

CHECKLIST FOR SCHOOL PERSONNEL INTERVIEWS

Name of Interviewer: _____

Instructions to Interviewer: Schedule a conference with an appropriate person from each administrative division of the school. If a specific service is not identified, discuss with the principal or assistant principal how the school provides the service to meet the needs of the students. Use the checklist to (1) formulate your questions and (2) ensure that you ask appropriate questions. You may add some of your own topics to the list. Check off each item for which you obtain an answer. Take notes in the space provided.

Guidance, Testing, Evaluation, and Reporting

Name of Person Interviewed: _____

Title of Person Interviewed: _____

Date, Time, and Place of Interview: _____

Approximate Length of Interview: _____

1. Purpose of guidance program
2. Procedures for obtaining services
3. Services of guidance program (individual and group)
4. Referral services
5. Services for pregnant students and single parents
6. Teachers' role in guidance
7. Students' role in guidance
8. Parents' role in guidance
9. Standardized tests and purpose
10. School's grading/reporting policies
11. School's promotion/retention policies
12. Academic advising and placing of students

Notes:

Library or Media Center/Instructional Materials and Equipment

Name of Person Interviewed: _____

Title of Person Interviewed: _____

Date, Time, and Place of Interview: _____

Approximate Length of Interview: _____

1. Available library materials related to subject and/or grade level
2. Library or media center hours for students and teachers
3. Procedures for using library or media center (class/students/teachers)
4. Vertical file and appropriate contents
5. Computer indexing of library materials
6. Equipment and media available for teachers' library/media center use
7. Checkout policies for students, teachers, and classes
8. Equipment and media available for classroom use
9. Procedures for instructing students in library/media center use
10. Assistance available for use of equipment and media
11. Availability and procedures for computer use by students and teachers
12. Procedures for selection and review of library materials and media

Notes:

Health Services

Name of Person Interviewed: _____

Title of Person Interviewed: _____

Date, Time, and Place of Interview: _____

Approximate Length of Interview: _____

1. Available health services at school
2. Services available through school referral
3. Sex education and condom distribution
4. Services for pregnant students
5. Procedures for teacher with ill/injured child
6. Procedures for dealing with HIV-positive student
7. School safety precautions, policies, and regulations
8. Other county/community services available to students
9. Health and related issues taught in classes

Notes:

Curriculum Resource Person or Assistant Principal for Curriculum

Name of Person Interviewed: _____

Title of Person Interviewed: _____

Date, Time, and Place of Interview: _____

Approximate Length of Interview: _____

1. School, district, county, or state curriculum guides
2. Multicultural aspects of the curriculum
3. School's organization for instruction:
   a. grouping
   b. departmentalization
   c. chain of command
   d. curricular offerings
   e. extra-curricular offerings
   f. scheduling for teachers and students
4. Planning requirements for teachers
5. In-service and other opportunities for teachers
6. Observation and evaluation of teachers
7. Procedures for selection and review of textbooks and classroom materials
8. Teachers' role in curriculum development and implementation
9. Community's role in curriculum development and implementation
10. Procedures for dealing with controversial issues and/or materials
11. Special education teachers
12. Reading teachers
13. Speech pathologists
14. Gifted program teachers
15. Social adjustment teachers, including drop-out prevention and in-school suspension
16. Dean of boys/girls
17. Music, art, and drama teachers
18. Other special teachers (bilingual, physical education)
19. Procedures for mainstreaming students

Notes:

Person in Charge of Student Discipline

Name of Person Interviewed: _____

Title of Person Interviewed: _____

Date, Time, and Place of Interview: _____

Approximate Length of Interview: _____

1. School policies/regulations regarding student behavior and appearance
2. Student handbook
3. Procedures for severe discipline referrals
4. Substance abuse programs
5. Drop-out prevention programs
6. School-administered discipline
7. Referrals to other agencies
8. Involvement of law enforcement in the school

Notes:

Principal or Assistant Principal

Name of Person Interviewed: _____

Title of Person Interviewed: _____

Date, Time, and Place of Interview: _____

Approximate Length of Interview: _____

1. School policies/regulations regarding teacher behavior and appearance.
2. Faculty handbook
3. Faculty meetings (time and how used)
4. Organizational pattern of local schools (i.e. board—central office—school)
5. Specialized type of school, such as magnet
6. Specialized programs, such as before-and after-school programs and preschool or childcare programs
7. Information about the community served by the school
8. Community and parent involvement in the school
9. Business involvement in the school
10. Professional organizations (i.e. union or academic)
11. Teachers' extra responsibilities
12. Student employment opportunities and procedures to follow

Notes:

FORM 16A

CHECKLIST OF COMPETENCIES

Name of Observer: _____

Date and Time of Observation: _____

Teacher: _____

School: _____

Instructions to the Observer: Using the list of competencies, goals, objectives, and/or performance indicators from a curriculum guide, develop your own ckecklist. (For an example of a checklist of competencies in a 7th grade math classroom, see p. 37.) If the competency, goal, objective and/or preference indicator is observed, place an "X" in the right-hand column.

Goals, Objectives, and/or Competencies	Performance Indicators	Observed

Competencies	Performance Indicators	Observed

FORM 17A

FORM FOR EXAMINING A CURRICULUM GUIDE

Examiner: _____

Date of Examination: _____

Objective: _____

_____

Instructions to the Examiner: Select a curriculum guide for the grade level and/or subject you will be observing. Complete this short answer survey.

1. Title of the guide: _____
2. Check one: The guide is from the school____; the school district____; the state____; other____ (specify)
3. Date of the guide: _____
4. Grade level(s) of the guide: _____
5. Subject area(s) of the guide: _____

_____

Answer the following yes/no or as indicated:

6. The guide includes: objectives____, student activities____, materials ____; resources____, examples____, bibliographies____, computer software sources____, test banks____, discussion questions____, material for making transparencies____, content outlines____, other (specify) _____
7. The guide suggests appropriate textbooks (specify): _____

_____

8. The guide suggests appropriate supplemental books._____
9. The guide suggests appropriate references. _____
10. The guide suggests activities for different levels of students (i.e. gifted, advanced, basic, etc.) _____

FORM 18A

SURVEY FOR EXAMINING A TEXTBOOK

Name of Examiner: _____

Date of Examination: _____

School: _____

Classroom Teacher: _____

Instructions to the Examiner: Complete the following either by writing X̲ in the response where appropriate, by checking the blank space where appropriate, or by checking either yes or no.

1. Title of text: _____

2. Author(s): _____

3. Publisher: _____

4. Year of publication: _____

5. Subject: _____

6. Grade level intended: _____

7. The text is part of a graded series. yes _____ no _____

8. Grade level(s) of the series (check one) K-6 _____; K-8 _____; K-12 _____; 6-8 _____; 9-12 _____; other (specify) _____

9. The text has the following aids: a) objectives, yes _____ no _____; b) marginal notes, yes _____ no _____; c) preview questions, yes _____ no _____; d) tables and figures, yes _____ no _____; e) illustrations, yes _____ no _____; f) index, yes _____ no _____; g) review questions, yes _____ no _____; h) glossary, yes _____ no _____; other _____

10. The teacher's manual for the text includes: a) lesson plans, yes _____ no _____; b) follow-up or supplementary activities, yes _____ no _____; c) transparencies, yes _____ no _____; d) duplicator masters, yes _____ no _____; e) tests, yes _____ no _____; f) resources, yes _____ no _____; g) other _____

11. Tables, figures, and illustrations: a) are placed near the content they support, yes _____ no _____; b) supplement the narrative, yes _____ no _____; c) reinforce the narrative, yes _____ no _____; d) are attractive and motivating, yes _____ no _____

12. Student workbooks, if provided, a) correlate with the text, yes ＿＿ no ＿＿; b) supplement the text, yes ＿＿ no ＿＿; provide effective directions, yes ＿＿ no ＿＿

13. The content of the text is organized by a) units, yes ＿＿ no ＿＿; themes, yes ＿＿ no ＿＿; b) topics, yes ＿＿ no ＿＿; c) chronological order, yes ＿＿ no ＿＿; d) skills, yes ＿＿ no ＿＿; e) objectives, yes ＿＿ no ＿＿; f) other ＿＿＿＿＿＿＿＿＿

14. The content of the text: a) is accurate, yes ____ no ____; b) relates to interests of students at this age level, yes ____ no ____; c) is readable by students of this age level, yes ____ no ____; d) is motivating to students of this age level, yes ____ no ____

15. The following content in the text relates to a curriculum guide either of the district, state, or school. List appropriate content below:

    _____, _____, _____

    _____, _____, _____

16. I would like to teach from this text: yes ____ no ____

17. Some comments and questions I would like to raise about this text are:

    _____

    _____

FORM 19A

CHECKLIST OF TECHNOLOGY/MEDIA
IN CLASSROOMS

Name of Observer: _____

Date of Observation: _____

School: _____

Classroom Teacher: _____

Grade/Subject: _____

Objective: _____

_____

Instructions to the Observer: After structured observation or an interview with the classroom teacher, put a check in the appropriate columns. Check if used with: I - Individual, SG - Small Group, WG - Whole Group.

Equipment	Number in Classroom	Stays in Classroom	Loaned from Media Center or Other Source	I/SG/WG
Projectors				
Overhead				
Slide				
Film				
Movie				
Opaque				
Tape Recorder(s)				
Computer(s)				
Record/ Cassette Player(s)				
T.V.				
Radio				
VCR				
Calculator(s)				
Software				
Typewriter(s)				
Others (list)				

FORM 20A

SOFTWARE SELECTION GUIDE FOR COMPUTER-ASSISTED INSTRUCTION

Examiner: _____

Date of Examination: _____

Software Title: _____

Publisher: _____

Date: _____

Instructional Purpose: _____

Computer Compatibility: _____

Directions to Examiner: Rate the content, usability, and design aspects of the instructional package on a scale of 1 to 5 (1 is lowest and 5 is highest).

A. CONTENT

_____ 1. Is the instructional content of the software appropriate to the established curriculum? (5th grade)

    _____ a. Does the subject matter of the software address educational objectives that are appropriate for the students who will use it?

    _____ b. Is the content accurate with no errors of fact or statement?

    _____ c. Is the content presented in an unbiased manner?

    _____ d. Is the program free of harmful generalizations and stereotypes based on sex, race, age, or culture?

_____ 2. Is the program interesting and enjoyable to use?

    _____ a. Is the instruction presented in a lively and interesting way?

    _____ b. Are the graphics, color, or sound pleasing and conducive to instruction?

    _____ c. Are program response times brief with a minimum of waiting time?

B. EDUCATIONAL DESIGN

_____ 1. Is the program clear and logically organized?

_____ 2. Can the user control the rate and type of instruction presented?

_____ 3. Does the program present the new concepts or skills to be learned in a meaningful context?

_____ 4. Does the program provide a sufficient amount of examples or illustrations to explain each new concept or skill?

_____ 5. Does the program lead to higher level understanding or application?

_____ 6. Does the program provide prompt instructional feedback?

_____ 7. Does the program evaluate the user's progress?

_____ 8. Do the evaluations allow diagnosis of the individual's weaknesses and strengths in the various instructional areas?

_____ 9. Can the evaluations be printed? (Y, N)

C. USABILITY

___   1.   Is the program easy to start and use?

___   2.   Is the program self-explanatory, not requiring dependence on a user's manual?

___   3.   Can the program disk be copied for multiple use? (Y, N)

___   4.   Is it easy to exit the program?

Designed by: James McGlinn, University of North Carolina at Asheville. Unpublished.

FORM 21A

CHECKLIST TO DETERMINE STUDENT ASSESSMENTS EMPLOYED IN THE CLASSROOM

Observer: _____

Teacher: _____

Grade/Subject: _____

School: _____

Date: _____

Objective: _____

_____

Instructions to Observer: After structured observation or interview with the classroom teacher, put a check in the appropriate column. *List additional assessments where required.

Type of Assessment	Observed	From Interview
1. Commercial Workbooks in Curricular Areas		
Reading		
Mathematics		
Science		
Social Studies		
Language Arts		
Others*		
2. Duplicated Sheets		
3. Homework Assignments		
4. Oral Presentation/Report		
5. Hands-On Performance		
Computer		
Science Experiment		
Construction Project		
Dramatic Performances/Skits		
Chalkboard Work		
Art Project		
Musical Production		
Classroom Displays/Bulletin Board		
School Displays		
Others*		

6. Written Work
   Reports
   Research Projects
   Creative Writing
   Others*

7. Teacher-Made Tests
8. Prepared Tests From Students' Texts
9. Standardized Tests
10. State Competency Tests
11. Anecdotal Records
    Writing Journals/Folders
    Art Folders
    Cumulative Record Folders
    Others*

12. Others*

FORM 22A

ANECDOTAL RECORD FOR OBSERVING STUDENTS

Name of Observer: _____

Date and Time of Observation: _____

Length of Observation: _____

Person and/or Event Observed: _____

Grade Level and/or Subject: _____

Objective of Observation: _____

_____

FORM 23A

SHADOWING FORM

Name of Shadowed Student: _____

Observer: _____

Date: _____

Time: _____

Grade: _____

Subjects: _____

Objective: _____

General Description of Location: _____

Instructions to the Observer: Select a student to shadow for an entire school day. Use a separate page for each class period or segment of the school day you observe. Every five to fifteen minutes, record what the subject of the observation is doing; also indicate what other students and teachers are doing. At the end of the day, summarize the shadowing. If possible, interview the student and report the results.

Subject/Class: _____

Time (recorded every five to fifteen minutes)	What Subject Was Doing	What Classmates and Teacher Were Doing

The following should be completed at the end of the shadowing:

Overview (summarize how the student seemed to be involved, how the student interacted with teachers and peers, what the student seemed to learn, how the student seems to feel about the class)

Report of interview with student:

FORM 24A

PROFILE CARD OF STUDENT

Observer's Name: _____

Student's Name: _____

Date: _____

Time: _____

Subject/Grade: _____

Location: _____

Number of Students Observed: _____

Time (recorded every minute)   **Student's Activities/Attitudes**

FORM 25A

DESCRIPTIVE PROFILE CHART

Plotted by: _____

Date: _____

Student Observed: _____

School: _____

Grade: _____

Interval: _____

Background: _____

Instructions to Observer: Record brief phrases to indicate the activities of the student during discussion and work periods. Place student activities under "application" if they show involvement in the lesson; place under "distraction" if they do not show involvement in the lesson.

Discussion Period		Work Period	
Application	**Distraction**	**Application**	**Distraction**

Adapted from John Devor, *The Experience of Student Teaching*, 1964.

FORM 26A

CODING SYSTEM TO OBSERVE STUDENT PARTICIPATION IN LESSONS

Observer: _____

Student: _____

Grade: _____

Date: _____

Topic: _____

Interval: _____

Directions: Place a slash in appropriate column to indicate student activities during a single lesson.

Important Contributions	**Minor Contributions**	**Distracting Remarks**

FORM 27A

INCOMPLETE SENTENCE INVENTORY

Observer's Name: _____

Student's Name: _____

Grade/Subject: _____

Date: _____

Objective: _____

Instructions to the Observer: Determine the purpose of completing an informal inventory. Then design some incomplete sentences related to your objective.

Instructions to the Student: Complete each sentence below as honestly and completely as possible. For example, you might complete number 1 as follows:

_____

_____.

_____

1.

2.

3.

4.

5.

6.

7.

8.

9.

10.

FORM 28A

TALLY CHART OF STUDENT GROUP SELECTIONS

Chosen Choosers																													
Chosen 1																													
2																													
3																													
Totals																													

From: Frederick J. McDonald, *Educational Psychology*, 2nd Ed., Wadsworth Publishing, 1965, p. 634.

FORM 29A

SOCIOGRAM BASED ON CHARTED STUDENT PREFERENCES

Directions to Observer: Using the tally chart of student group selections, put the names of those students selected most in a prominent place on the page. Identify males by placing name in a circle, females by placing names in boxes. Then put names of students selected by these few next to them. If they selected each other, connect them with a dotted line. If not, draw an arrow to the student selected. Proceed in this fashion until all names are represented on the form.

FORM 30A

ANECDOTAL RECORD OF PRETEACHING ACTIVITIES

Name of Student Participant: _____

Name of Teacher: _____

Grade Level and/or Subject: _____

Date: _____

Objective: _____

Directions to Student Participant: Keep an account of the activities you participated in prior to actual teaching. Indicate how you felt about each day's events.

FORM 31A

CHECKLIST OF ROUTINES FOR HELPING THE TEACHER

Name of Student Participant: _____

Name of Teacher: _____

Grade Level and/or Subject: _____

Date: _____

Objective: _____

_____

Instructions to Student Participant: All the duties listed below are important to the management of the instructional environment. You will need to learn to complete these simultaneously with teaching the students and managing the class. To help you learn to do so efficiently, complete all tasks appropriate to your teaching situation and indicate the date each is accomplished. Please have the classroom teacher sign this form when all appropriate activities have been successfully completed.

Activity   **Date Completed**

1. Make a seating chart.
2. Take attendance.
3. Run errands for the classroom teacher.
4. Help with classroom housekeeping.
5. Organize materials needed for a lesson.
6. Make copies of materials needed for the lesson.
7. Help pass out materials to the students.
8. Arrange a bulletin board.
9. Check out books from the library to be used by students in the classroom.
10. Check out media to be used in a lesson.
11. Make a chart or graph.
12. Make a transparency or stencil.
13. Run a film, filmstrip, videotape, etc.
14. Get supplementary materials needed for a lesson (e.g., magazine illustrations, pamphlets, maps, etc.)
15. Develop a bibliography for an upcoming unit.
16. Correct papers.
17. Set up or help set up a lab.
18. Write news/assignments on the chalkboard.
19. Set up a learning center.
20. Set up an experiment or a demonstration.

21. Obtain a speaker to come to class or help organize a class field trip.
22. Help gather materials for a class party.
23. Help make costumes for a class play.
24. Send out a class newsletter to parents.
25. Other (please list below):

I certify that the student participant listed above has successfully completed all of the above activities that are appropriate to my classroom.

_____

(Classroom teacher's signature)

FORM 32A

CHECKLIST OF ROUTINES INVOLVING STUDENTS

Name of Student Participant: _____

Name of Teacher: _____

Grade Level and/or Subject: _____

Date: _____

Objective: _____

_____

Instructions to Student Participant: All the activities listed below are important to the instruction of the students. You will need to learn to complete these simultaneously with teaching the students and managing the class. To help you learn to do so efficiently, complete all tasks appropriate to your teaching situation and indicate the date each is accomplished. Please have the classroom teacher sign this form when all appropriate activities have been successfully completed.

Activity	Date Completed
1. Orient a new student.	
2. Help individual students with seat work.	
3. Work with a club or student activity.	
4. Assist a small group.	
5. Work with an individual student in a lab (e.g., computer, language, science).	
6. Assist a handicapped student.	
7. Assist students with library research.	
8. Monitor a test.	
9. Collect money.	
10. Hand out and collect materials.	
11. Listen to an individual student read or recite a lesson.	
12. Give a test or a quiz.	
13. Assist young children with clothing.	
14. Bring books or materials to share with the students.	
15. Supervise students outside the classroom.	
16. Read aloud or tell a story.	
17. Help students in a learning center.	
18. Accompany students to a school office, the bus, or the playground.	
19. Attend a parent-teacher conference.	

20. Work with the teacher in developing an IEP (Individual Education Plan) for a mainstreamed student.
21. Accompany students to before- or after-school programs.
22. Help monitor the hallway, lunchroom, or playground.
23. Other (please list below):
Worked with small groups in computer lab for 30 minutes, two days a week.

I certify that the student participant listed above has successfully completed all of the above activities that are appropriate to my classroom.

_____
(Classroom teacher's signature)

FORM 33A

LESSON PLAN

Name of Student Participant: _____

Name of Teacher: _____

Grade Level/Subject Area: _____

Date: _____

Goal: _____

Objectives: _____

_____

_____

_____

_____

Materials: _____

_____

_____

_____

Duration: _____

Instructions to the Student Participant: Whether your plan covers several classroom sessions or only one, each lesson should include the steps listed below.

1. Anticipatory Set:

2. Objective:

3. Teacher Input:

4. Checking for Understanding:

5. Guided Practice:

6. Independent Practice:

7. Closure:

FORM 33B

DAILY LESSON PLAN FORMAT

Subject/Grade: _____   Name: _____

Topic: _____   Date: _____

Specific Content of Lesson

Lesson Objectives(s)

Procedures

Materials

Evaluation

Key Words or Ideas

FORM 33C

LESSON PLAN FORMAT

Text Reference _____

Objectives: _____

Activity	Description of Activities and Setting	Materials and Supplies	Time
1. Focus and Review			
2. State of Objectives			
3. Teacher Input			
4. Guided Practice			
5. Independent Practice			
6. Closure			

Resources:

FORM 34A

UNIT PLAN FORMAT

Name of Student Participant: _____

Name of Teacher: _____

Grade Level/Subject Area: _____

Date: _____

Topic: _____

Duration: _____

1. Introduction (What will be covered in this unit; why is it important? Brief statement about the nature and scope of the unit; its significance and justification; concepts, issues, skills or activities that will be covered):

2. Objectives or anticipated outcomes (What do I expect the students to accomplish; what changes in behavior do I envision; what will each student be doing to demonstrate the achievement and/or change in behavior?):

3. Instructional aids or resources (What do I need to teach this unit? List all materials, supplies, audiovisual and/or equipment needed. Identify paperbacks, newspapers, magazines, games, texts, etc., to be used as part of or supplemental to the unit. Relying solely on the classroom textbook is not advisable):

4. Content (curriculum) outline (When and what am I going to teach? Outline topics, subtopics, problems, concepts, issues, ideas, information, and/or skills involved, activities to be utilized and approximate time involved for each activity):

using a computer program, using a table of contents, reading a textbook for meaning, cutting out objects, using a microscope, etc.) List the skill(s) you taught:

2. Diagnosing a student's strength or weakness (e.g., administering a specific individual test, listening to a student read, asking a student questions on a variety of levels, watching a student do a mathematical computation, observing a student using a computer program, watching a student use a piece of equipment, etc.). List the method(s) you employed and what you were attempting to diagnose:

3. Remedying a weakness (e.g., helping a student learn to cut out a shape with scissors, assisting a student with rules of phonics or grammar, drilling a student on vocabulary, showing a student how to find meaning in a paragraph, demonstrating for a student how to use a piece of equipment safely, etc.). List the method(s) you employed and the weakness you were attempting to remedy:

4. Developing a special talent (e.g., teaching a student a technique of drawing, reading a piece of student writing and providing support and suggestions, listening to a student writing and providing support and suggestions, listening to a

student read and discussing what has been read, talking to a student about a historical event, working with a student on a science project, helping a student complete a woodworking project, teaching basic computer programming, taking the student to a museum, etc.). List the method(s) you employed and the talent you were attempting to develop:

5. Other (List specific long-range tutoring activities in which you have participated):

Comment on what you learned from these activities:

I certify that the student participant listed above has successfully completed those tutoring activities indicated above.

_____

(Classroom teacher's signature)

FORM 37A

T TORING PLANNING CHECKLIST

Name of Student Particip t: _____

Name of Pupil Tutored: __ _____

Name of Teacher: _____ _____

Date: _____ _____

Objective: _____ _____

_____   _____

Instructions to Tutor: As you comple each of the following in your tutoring plans, indicate the date completed.

Planning Activity   **Date Completed**

1. Discuss the student you will tutor wit he classroom teacher.
2. Discuss possible tutoring topics and tech ues with the classroom teacher.
3. Carefully plan an initial "getting-to-know-y " session with the student.
4. Diagnose student strengths and weaknesses a ecessary.
5. Check available curriculum guides to determin ills to be taught and their sequence.
6. Set a specific objective for each tutoring session.
7. Develop a plan for each tutoring session (appropri plan formats can be found on pp. 148, 150, and 151, and chapter 5, pp. 77–79).
8. Consult appropriate resources for teaching techniques materials.
9. Make sure all necessary materials are available and copie prior to each tutoring session.
10. Monitor the pupil's progress by keeping a log of each day's tutoring.
11. Discuss student's progress with the classroom teacher. Ask for additional suggestions for helping the student.

FORM 38A

PRE-PLANNING SMALL GROUP CHECKLIST

Name of Student Participant: _____

Name of Teacher: _____

Grade Level/Subject Area: _____

Date: _____

Objective: _____

_____

Instructions to Student Participant: As you complete each of the following in planning for your small group, indicate the date completed.

Pre-planning Activity   **Date Completed**

1. Discuss possible types of small-group teaching with the classroom teacher.
2. Discuss the assignment of students to the small group.
3. Discuss the classroom teacher's goal for the small group.
4. Consider the needs, interests, and abilities of the students who will participate in the instructional group. Discuss with the classroom teacher.
5. Develop an assessment tool or technique that can measure the progress of several students simultaneously (e.g., students complete mathematics problems that begin slightly below their level of achievement and continue beyond their level of achievement; students answer questions about reading samples that are below their reading level and continue beyond their reading level; students complete multiple-choice items on a leveled vocabulary list; students attempt to perform part of a one-act play; students read parts orally in a short play; etc.).
6. Determine a specific objective for each small-group session.
7. Develop a plan for each small-group session (appropriate plan formats can be found on pp. 148, 150, and 151, and in chapter 5, pp. 77–79).
8. Consult appropriate resources for teaching techniques and materials.
9. Make sure all necessary materials are available and copied prior to each small-group session.
10. Monitor the pupils' progress by having them complete individual practice exercises related to each session's objective.
11. Discuss the students' progress with the classroom teacher. Ask for additional suggesitons for helping the students.

FORM 39A

SMALL-GROUP TEACHING CHECKLIST

Name of Student Participant: _____

Name of Teacher: _____

Grade Level/Subject Area: _____

Topic: _____

Date: _____

Objective: _____

_____

Instructions to Student Participant: Use this checklist as you prepare to teach and during your teaching of your small group. To be sure that your lesson includes each of the following, check each item off as it occurs.

Teaching Activity	Appears in Lesson

1. The students' attention is grabbed.
2. The objective of the lesson is related to the students.
3. Prerequisite knowledge is ascertained through questions and answers, a quiz, completion of an exercise, etc.
4. If appropriate, gaps in needed information are filled in.
5. New information, skills, or materials are presented through explanation, demonstration, discussion, etc.
6. Individual tasks are assigned each group member.
7. Student performance is elicited and monitored through independent work.
8. Teacher feedback is provided to each student.
9. Student work is related to previous and future learning.
10. Students review what they have learned in the lesson.
11. The objective for the next small-group lesson is determined and communicated to the students.

FORM 40A

SAMPLE CHECKLIST FOR WORKING WITH LARGE GROUPS

Name of Student Participant: _____

Name of Teacher: _____

Grade Level/Subject Area: _____

Date: _____

Objective: _____

_____

Instructions to Student Participant: As you complete each of these activities, check it off in the right-hand column.

Activity   **Completed**

Management of the Classroom
1. Discuss management rules with the classroom teacher.
2. Ascertain consequences for infractions with the classroom teacher.
3. Use only the discipline methods sanctioned by the classroom teacher and the school.
4. Communicate the rules and consequences to the students so that they know you will enforce them.
5. Enforce rules and apply consequences consistently.
6. Do not threaten if you do not intend to carry through on the threat (e.g., "If you aren't quiet, I'll keep you all after school").
7. Make eye contact with as many students as possible.
8. Call students by name. (Make a temporary seating chart to help you learn names or have the students make, wear, or display name tags.)

Teaching
1. Carefully plan lessons and divide them into clear segments (use a planning format such as those provided on pp. 148, 150, and 151, and in chapter 5, pp. 77–79).
2. Be sure all materials are copied and ready to distribute.
3. Preview all materials prior to using or showing.
4. Preread anything you intend to use.
5. Maintain instructional momentum (keep up the pace; do not spend too long on any one element of the plan; do not over-explain).
6. Be certain that students understand what is expected (e.g., ask them to explain to you what they are to do; place assignments on the chalkboard prior to the lesson; make sure instructions and printing on handouts are clear; provide clear examples).

7. Be sure students know how to and are capable of accomplishing the task (e.g., beware of asking students to do tasks for which they do not have prerequisite knowledge or skills; check with the classroom teacher to be sure they will be able to accomplish what you expect).

8. Review previous lessons and prerequisite knowledge or skills required for this lesson.

9. Actively involve the students in the lesson.

10. Use teaching methodology appropriate to the subject and the maturity of the students (e.g., labs in science classes, oral reading and independent writing in English and language arts, problem solving in mathematics, research in social studies, etc.).

11. Employ a variety of teaching techniques so that all types of learners can achieve (e.g., audiovisuals, hands-on activities, problem solving, student-designed charts and graphs, laboratories, demonstrations, etc.).

12. Assess students' level of mastery of skills and concepts as often as possible (e.g., class work that requires demonstration of mastery, observation of students completing classwork, homework that is not merely drill, quizzes, journal entries, writing assignments, etc.).

13. Expect mastery of skills and concepts after a period of teaching, practice, coaching, assessing, reteaching, practice, coaching, etc.

14. Do not expect all students to master all concepts and skills in the same way or at the same time. Group students to provide additional assistance to those who have not mastered important concepts and skills. Use different teaching techniques with these students, or allow those who have mastered the skills or concepts to tutor those who have not.

REFERENCES

Amidon, E. J., and Flanders, N. A. 1963. *The role of the teacher in the classroom.* Minneapolis, MN: Paul S. Amidon and Associates.

Anderson, G. J. 1973. *The assessment of learning environments: A manual for the learning environment inventory and the class inventory.* Halifax, Nova Scotia: Atlantic Institute of Education.

Anderson, L. 1991. *Student Teaching Journal.* University of North Carolina at Asheville. (Unpublished manuscript).

Austin-Martin, G., Bull, D., and Molrine, C. 1981. A study of the effectiveness of a pre-student teaching experience in promoting positive attitudes toward teaching. *Peabody Journal of Education, 58* (3), 148–153.

Bloom, B., Ed. 1956. *Taxonomy of educational objectives: The classification of educational goals. Handbook I: Cognitive domain.* New York: Longman S. Green and Company.

Borich, G. D. 1990. *Observation skills for effective teaching.* Columbus, OH: Merrill.

Brown, T. 1968. *Student teaching in a secondary school,* 2nd ed. New York: Harper and Row.

Cooper, J. M., Ed. 1982. *Classroom teaching skills,* 2nd ed. Lexington, MA: D. C. Heath.

Crow, L., and Crow, A. 1965. *The student teacher in the elementary school.* New York: David McKay.

Gagne, R. M., and Briggs, L. 1979. *Principles of instructional design.* New York: Holt, Rinehart and Winston.

Grambs, J., and Carr, J. C. 1979. *Modern methods in secondary education.* New York: Holt, Rinehart and Winston.

Harris, L. 1985. *The Metropolitan Life survey of former teachers.* New York: Metropolitan Life.

Henry, M. 1988. The effect of increased exploratory field experiences upon the perceptions and performance of student teachers. In *Action in teacher education: Tenth-year anniversary issue, commemorative edition,* Ed. J. Sikula, 93–97. Reston, VA: Association of Teacher Educators.

Hunter, M. 1984. Knowing, teaching, and supervising. In *Using what we know about teaching: 1984 Yearbook of Association for Supervision and Curriculum Development,* Ed. P. Hofford, 169–203. Alexandria, VA: Association for Supervision and Curriculum Development.

_____. 1985a. Building effective elementary schools. In *Education on trial,* Ed. W. J. Johnson, 53–67. San Francisco, CA: ICS Press.

_____. 1985b. What's wrong with Madeline Hunter? *Educational Leadership, 42* (6), 57–60.

Joyce, J. 1991. *Student Teaching Journal.* University of North Carolina at Asheville. (Unpublished manuscript).

Kounin, J. S. 1970. *Discipline and group management in classrooms.* New York: Holt, Rinehart and Winston.

McDonald, F. J. 1965. *Educational psychology,* 2nd ed. Belmont, CA: Wadsworth.

Moffett, J., and Wagner, B. J. 1983. *Student-centered language arts and reading, K–13: A handbook for teachers,* 3rd ed. Boston, MA: Houghton Mifflin.

North Carolina Department of Public Instruction, 1979. *Competency goals and performance indicators, K–12.* Raleigh, NC: Author.

_____. 1986. *Performance appraisal program,* Raleigh, NC: Author (Unpublished manuscript).

Parsons, T. and Shills, E., Eds. 1951. *Toward a general theory of action.* Cambridge, MA: Harvard University Press.

Perkins, H. V. 1969. *Human development and learning.* Belmont, CA: Wadsworth.

Raines, S., and Isenberg, J. 1991. Instructional record form research roundtable: Reflective practice. *Newsletter for the Journal of Early Childhood Education* (Winter) 12 (1), 25.

Reed, A. J. S., and Bergemann, V. E. 1992. *In the classroom: An introduction to education.* Guilford, CT: The Dushkin Publishing Group.

Sander, N. M. 1966. *Classroom questions: What kinds?* New York: Harper and Row.

Sharan, S., and Sharan, Y. 1976. *Small group teaching.* Englewood Cliffs, NJ: Educational Technology Publications.

Sprinthall, L. 1986. An adapted Madeline Hunter lesson plan. In *A strategy guide for teachers: Guidebook for supervisors of novice teachers,* Raleigh: Department of Curriculum and Instruction, College of Education and Psychology, North Carolina State University. (Unpublished manuscript).

Stanford, G. 1977. *Developing effective classroom groups: A practical guide for teachers.* New York: Hart.

Sunal, D. 1976. *A comparison of two pre-professional programs in the department of early childhood elementary education.* University of Maryland (ERIC Document Reproduction Service No. ED 139 624).

Ur, P. 1981. *Discussions that work: Task-centered fluency practice.* Cambridge, UK: Cambridge University Press.

Walberg, H., and Anderson, G. 1968. Classroom climate and individual learning. *Journal of Educational Psychology, 59* (6), 414–419.

Weber, W. 1982. Classroom management. In *Classroom teaching skills,* Ed. J. M. Cooper, Lexington, MA: D. C. Heath.